Angels
Barbarians
and
Nincompoops

Angels

Barbarians

and

Nincompoops

...and a lot of
other words
you *thought*
you knew

Anthony Esolen

TAN Books
Charlotte, NC

Cover design by David Ferris Design

Library of Congress Cataloging-in-Publication Data

Names: Esolen, Anthony M., author.
Title: Angels, barbarians, and nincompoops : ...and a lot of other words you thought you knew / Anthony Esolen.
Description: Charlotte, North Carolina : TAN Books, [2017]
Identifiers: LCCN 2016055491 (print) | LCCN 2017002862 (ebook) | ISBN 9781505108743 (hardcover) | ISBN 9781505108750 (ePub) | ISBN 9781505108767 (Mobi)
Subjects: LCSH: Vocabulary. | English language--Glossaries, vocabularies, etc.
Classification: LCC PE1449 .E85 2017 (print) | LCC PE1449 (ebook) | DDC 428.1--dc23
LC record available at https://lccn.loc.gov/2016055491

Published in the United States by
TAN Books
P. O. Box 410487
Charlotte, NC 28241
www.TANBooks.com

Printed and bound in the United States of America

Test Your Knowledge Before and After

The following four quizzes are to be taken before and after reading the book. If you don't do better the second time than the first, you must buy a second copy of the book and take all four quizzes a third time. Answers are found at the back. Good luck!

....

Quiz One: Find the Oddball

In each of the following groups of three words, one of them is *not etymologically related* to the other two, even if they may mean the same thing. Can you guess which one? (*Etymology is the study of the origin of words. We don't want anyone looking skyward and exclaiming, "But none of these are insects!"*)

1. square, queer, quarter
2. daily, diurnal, Zeus
3. pork, farrow, swine
4. most, foremost, former
5. host, guest, ghost
6. foil, boil, bole
7. pastor, food, farmer
8. ring (on your finger), circle, round
9. war, guerilla, worth
10. communion, a, union

Quiz Two:
Fictionary

For each of the following, guess whether the suggested relation is genuine or a joke:

1. *Too* is related to *to,* because when you add something to a pile or a list, you add it *to* it.
2. *Beyond the pale* means you aren't even *pale* anymore; you are a dead white.
3. *Pulling out the stops* means that you pull out all the knobs on a pipe organ, because when the knobs are in, they stop up the air.
4. *Expect* is related to *expectorate,* because you are hoping for something in your heart, that is, your chest.
5. *Parchment* is related to *parch,* because of the heating of the sheepskin required in its manufacture.
6. *It likes me* originally meant *I like it.*
7. *Mart* originally meant not the place where you bought something, but the cow you would buy.
8. *Unkempt* means that you aren't *kempt,* that is, you haven't combed your hair.
9. *Prissy* comes from *pristine,* with the sense of fussy neatness.
10. *Sex* is related to *seek,* for obvious reasons.

Quiz Three:
Antique, or Cheap Imitation?

Which of the following forms really used to be standard in English?

1. eat, past tense of *eat,* pronounced *et*
2. snuck, past tense of *sneak*
3. span, past tense of *spin*
4. kine, plural of *cow*
5. arn, instead of *ran*
6. brang, past tense of *bring*
7. busted, past tense of *bust*
8. grice, plural of *grouse*
9. ment, past tense of *mend*
10. lamben, plural of *lamb*

....

Quiz Four:
You've Got to Be Kidding!

True or False:

1. Pirates outfielder Paul Waner was nicknamed "Big Poison" by a fan with a Brooklyn accent, who really meant "Big Person."
2. A bum is so called because he has a fat one.
3. "Anchors away" should be "anchors aweigh," meaning that you "weigh" or pull up the anchor.

4. A touchdown is so called because the player used to touch the football to the ground once he got to the end zone.

5. Jibber-jabber is what schoolboys used to call *algebra* when they didn't understand it.

6. You get "the vapors" because somebody has to get out the smelling salts to revive you.

7. A "humorous" person might be someone whose liver is producing an unusual amount of bile.

8. A "pig in a poke" was a piglet in a sack, all tied up.

9. To send something "up the gut" is like sending a ship into a narrow strait.

10. "Ye" is slang for "you," by analogy with "we."

....

Author's Note

Unless otherwise noted, Biblical quotations are from the Douay-Rheims Bible. The King James version is used where its masterly English is essential for my purposes. Where Biblical citations are noted in parentheses using the term "see," the scripture verse in question was recalled or paraphrased.

The passages from Dante are my own translations as they appear in the *Inferno*, *Purgatory*, and *Paradise* published by Modern Library (Translation, introduction, and notes copyright © 2002, 2003, 2004 respectively by Random House, Inc.).

How to Read *This* Book
(. . . and a law to help you do so)

With apologies to the great Mortimer Adler and his more ambitious tome entitled *How To Read A Book* ("A" in the sense of "any" or "every". . . . The bold A is our own for emphasis; we don't think it appears in Adler's title), we offer our readers these more humble instructions with regards to *this* book. Don't do it all at once. Linger over it. Peruse it at your leisure. Read the entries one per day if you like, perhaps while engaging in a daily activity, such as, well, brushing your teeth. And, to help you derive the most enjoyment and erudition, both philological and theological, therefrom, we offer the following law to bear in mind. Trust us . . . it comes up a lot.

....

Grimm's Law

Yes, it's the Jakob Grimm of the Fairy Tales. The Law says: *Thou shalt not enter a gingerbread house.* Actually, it doesn't say that. It is a law associating consonants in the Germanic languages with consonants in Proto-Indo-European, which was the language that Proto-Indo-Europeans spoke, our ancestors from the steppes of Eurasia. Those ancestors of ours were an energetic bunch. They fanned out everywhere, north, west, and south, and ended up in places where we might not think we had any relations. The people of Iran do not speak an Arabic language, and the people of India do not speak an Indo-Chinese language: Iranians speak Farsi, a distant cousin of English, and Indians speak Bengali, same thing. Anyway, to give one example, Grimm's Law tells us that if we have a Germanic word beginning with *h*, we should look for a Latin or Greek word beginning with *c* (*k*). Particular applications of the law will be noted as they come up.

INTRODUCTION

"What's in a name?" asks Juliet, who wishes that Romeo were not a Montague, so that she might marry him and not incur the anger of her father and the rest of her Montague-hating family. But the scholastic philosophers said that names followed upon the things they named, and so words help to reveal the essences of things. A rose by any other name would smell as sweet, but perhaps an ill-chosen name would not help us recall the fragrance of the rose when the flower itself was not before us.

We're the creators and the creatures of words: we use them even when we are not speaking or reading. We dream in words. When we encounter a reality that leaves us speechless, we say, "Words cannot describe it!" And then we go ahead and try to do so anyway. When we meet a new thing, we take upon ourselves the primeval privilege of Adam, and give a name to it. Small children love nothing better than to point at a thing and give it the right name.

In days of yore (and just what is "yore"?), young children had to learn about the innards of our words, because they learned grammar and were expected to venture forth upon another language, often Latin. In our day, they do neither, so they end up being the tools of words rather than artisans who use them. Silly and empty slogans slap at us over and over, like waves that lift and float a jellyfish.

This is too bad, because then we become easy prey for the slogan-masters, who themselves are not usually conscious of what they are doing. And yet there remains in us a fascination with words, a delight in them when they are strange or slippery or comical or formidable; and twelve to twenty years of schooling is insufficient to spoil it utterly. We hear that the word for *bat* in German is *Fliedermaus,* a mouse on wings, and it strikes us as exactly right, even amiable, if anything about that critter can be. We hear that *spaghetti* in Italian really means *little strings,* and we say, "Of course!" And we imagine a child asking his mother whether they can have strings and meatballs for supper.

Words also bring history out of the books and onto the tips of our tongues as it were. Why do speakers of English walk down *Main Street?* Because England was invaded by the Normans, who spoke French, that's why. It's why we eat veal (French), beef (French), and pork (French), rather than calf, steer, and swine. We hear that people in those same yore-days did not really love their spouses, because people married for money rather than for love. Someone should have relayed that news to all the speakers of English who made up so many words like *sweetheart* and *darling:* the latter really *dear-ling,* the one who is dear, precious, close to your heart.

And sometimes the history stretches back into pre-history. We have no records of our Indo-European ancestors who lived on those steppes of Eurasia. They were not literate. But they sure were on the move. They migrated everywhere, and their original language developed into scores of others, all related, like the limbs and branches of a great-trunked tree. What do people from India, Iran, Armenia, Latvia, Norway, France, Italy, Greece, England, and Germany have in common with the ancient Hittites? That distant ancestral language. In that sense Lars from Sweden is closer to Reza from Iran than he is to Timo from Finland, just across the Baltic Sea—for Finnish, like Hungarian and Basque, happens *not* to be in our big family.

Words also reveal us to ourselves. The makers of words are like artists who leave the impress of their personalities on the art. Or, since children are energetic word-makers, we might say that we dabble in painting word-pictures and get our fingerprints all over them. I'm not talking about poets and playwrights here. I'm talking about everyone. Why do flowers become the names of girls: Daisy, Lily, Rose, Violet? Why do men in groups, whether English or Italian or Latin or Hebrew, call themselves "boys"? Why do all languages have a way of expressing not what is or was or will be, but what *might have been* or *would have been,* but isn't?

My purpose in this book is very modest. I want only to whet the appetite. Take the following as a hundred or so *jeux d'esprit*—wonderful French phrase! They are short essays on words, tossed off in a spirit of play. I hope to encourage the reader to want to learn more about words in general and our own language in particular, confident that a love of words may well lead us down one of the more amiable paths towards *the Word, through Whom all things were made.*

THE WORDS

If you come from southern Massachusetts and drop your post-vocalic r's, you might describe your mammar's mammar as *grammar*—as the Massachusetts girls in *Little Women* call their mommy Marmie. But for most people the word *grammar* describes a small grab bag of arbitrary "rules" nobody really understands or remembers. For the few and the proud, however, it denotes the structural logic of a language, made manifest in rules or tendencies that really do make sense—since making sense, after all, is what language is for. When I ask my college freshmen whether they studied grammar in high school, most of them tell me that they did, but when I go on to ask them what a participle is, they give me a sheepish look, and admit that maybe they didn't study it after all. That's the truth, right there; they didn't and they haven't. To learn English "grammar" as that grab bag is like studying "zoology" by examining a dog's tail, the eating habits of cows, and what worms do when you cut them in half. There's no coherence to it, no systematic analysis, no way to grasp the whole.

I aim to supply some of that lack in these essays, while having some fun. For anyone who wants to write or speak well should get to know the stuff of their craft, just as painters should get their fingers sticky in colors.

Back to the word *grammar*: it comes to us nearly intact from the Greek *grammatike,* the study of letters. That word comes from the verb *graphein, to write.* That didn't mean typing things onto a screen, as I am doing now. It meant taking a stylus and carving letters into a tablet; rather strenuous labor, which is why people often employed secretaries to carve their letters (and their letters) into the clay. The Greek word is cousin to the Anglo-Saxon *ceorfan* (pronounced *CHEH-or-van*), *to carve, to cut.* In the old days that verb was "strong," meaning that it formed its principle parts by changing the vowel: *ceorfan, cearf, curfon, corven;* the last, the past participle, survives in the good old adjective *carven.*

I am quite fond of our English word for the birth of the Lord, *Christmas.* It's one of a host of old mass-words which provide abundant evidence that our English forefathers measured their seasons by the liturgical year. There's Christmas, but also *Candlemas,* the feast of the Presentation of the baby Jesus in the temple, on

February 2, the fortieth day after His birth. There's *Lammas,* an English harvest festival on August 1 (the name comes from the title Lamb of God); *Michaelmas,* the feast of Saint Michael the Archangel, on September 29; and *Martinmas* or *Martlemas,* the feast of Saint Martin of Tours, on November 11. Martin was a Roman soldier who gave up his life in the army and became a monk and, eventually, the Bishop of Tours. I've been told that his feast was chosen by the combatants at the end of World War I as most appropriate for the armistice that was supposed to end all wars.

Most of the European languages have words for Christmas that refer specifically to the Savior's *birth,* from the Latin adjective *natalis:* Italian *Natale,* French *Noël,* Welsh *Nadolig;* or from the Latin noun *nativitas:* Spanish *Navidad.* German, though, has *Weihnachten,* literally *Hallowed Night* (*weihen,* to consecrate); the emphasis is upon the birth of Him who would sacrifice Himself for us. The Scandinavian countries have variants upon what we know as Yule: Swedish *Jul.* That was an old pagan feast, taken over by the Christians when they converted the Germans in the northlands. That Scandinavian word made its way across the North Sea and the English Channel into France—recall, Normandy: the peninsula where the North-men live, that is, the Vikings. There the word took root as French *jolif, mirth (fit for Yuletide);* and entered English as *jolly,* which had an odd history of its own, sometimes having more to do with lusty youth than with an old elf with a round belly.

Yes, our ancestors reckoned their time by the Savior, and the saints, and the stars. We, by digits turning on a dial, without meaning. God bless our ancestors, wiser than we!

*a*ngel

For every person who reads good books or cherishes great art, there's a different and highly personal measuring-rod for the decline of western civilization. What's happened to angels may serve as well as any. The *malach* of Scripture is a mighty and awe-striking herald of God. He is *Michael, Who is like God?*, wielding his sword and dispatching the dragon to perdition below. He is *Gabriel,* God is strong, or the affable *Raphael,* God heals, who in the person of Azariah accompanies the boy Tobias on his long and fruitful journey, and returns with the fish gall that will heal the eyes of his blind father. C. S. Lewis captures the strangeness and the power of the angels in his Space Trilogy, and then of course there is the incomparable Milton. More from Milton to come; much more.

The other day I happened (in *The Century,* 1885) upon a black and white lithograph of *The Angel with the Flaming Sword*, by a late nineteenth century painter named Edwin Blashford. The angel is standing at guard, holding the sword in front of him, point down, against the earth. The fire of the blade lights him from below, shining upon his face and his bare chest. He is young, pure, grave, and powerfully built, on the verge of manhood. I searched for the image on the internet and found it; and along with it, another image of the angel with the flaming sword—a sluttish female in an iron bra and a leather bikini, the creature of somebody's grubby imagination.

So it goes. Our word *angel* comes from Old English *engel*, from Latin *angelus*, borrowed from Greek *angelos*, meaning *messenger*. "Behold, it is the herald of the Lord!" cries Virgil to Dante in the dawning twilight of Purgatory: *"Ecco l'angel di Dio!"* That's how one translator I know well renders it. The bureaucrats who sat heavy upon the soul of Scripture, lying like lead within its bosom as they translated it from Greek into the Unglish of a certain version I dislike intensely and will not name, turned up their noses at *angel* or *herald*. They say that a *messenger* came from God to Abraham on Mount Moriah, which in our tongue makes him sound like a telegraph boy from Western Union. "God to Abraham: stop. Hands off the boy. Stop. Faithfulness duly noted. Stop."

Lovers of beauty in language and liturgy to such translators: STOP!

tidings

"Time and tide wait for no man," says the old proverb. It's a nice alliterative pair, those two, and we may be led to think that the words are related, since the *tide* notoriously comes in on *time*. But they aren't.

The word *time* comes into English through French, after the Norman invasion in 1066, when William the Conqueror unloaded into English harbors whole boatloads of surplus words, and instead of throwing them overboard as the patriots did with the tea in Boston, the English people started to use them, and, *voilà!* We end up with French words everywhere we look: *place, large, chief, munch, main, very, money, pay, people.* English is a language with Germanic topsoil, French fertilizer, and mulch from everywhere. We have more words, far more, and from a wider variety of sources, than any other language in the world. Our *time* is French *temps,* Latin *tempus.*

Old English *tid* (with a long *i,* pronounced *teed*) meant *time,* not as duration but as instance. So, if you wanted to say, "That time I decked him," *tid* was your word. It was applied to the waves for the obvious reason that they are at their highest and their lowest at certain instances: hence, the *tides,* which of course you'd want to know about if you were going down to the sea in ships, or even if you were fishing in a small boat off shore. A *spring tide* is not a watery surge in April: it is literally the *jumping tide,* the high tide when sun and moon have aligned to make our water bulge upwards the most and overspill the sides of its container.

So if you want to know what has happened or what is happening right now, you're asking not about the *timing,* which has to do with the passing hour as such, but about the *tidings.* The angel to the shepherds: "I bring you good tidings of great joy" (Lk 2:10). The word kept its pride of place in German: *Zeit, time.* You read the *Zeitung,* the newspaper, to get the *tidings.* Whether they're tidings of great joy is another matter. We in English, meanwhile, read or say we read *The Times,* let us say *The New York Times,* to find out what its editors and writers want to persuade us is happening around the world.

Catholic

On an airplane recently I read an interesting article about the educational efforts of Marianist fathers beginning in Meiji Japan, in the late nineteenth century, and continuing into the time of the second Sino-Japanese war. The fathers kept religious instruction carefully separate from instruction in the other subjects, not because they believed that the faith did not bear upon those others, but because they wanted to win the trust of the wary Japanese officials and the intelligentsia. Even so, they won quite a few notable converts who became scientists, military generals, politicians, and professors, and they defended the virtue of patriotism, bound up with Japan's ambition to be the head of an east Asian alliance. Then came Pearl Harbor. The article ended there.

In Japanese pronunciation, they are *katorikku*, which is entirely understandable. The consonant in *catholic* that we spell with the two letters *th* is a sound that does not exist in Japanese. Nor, for that matter, will you find it in Chinese, Hawaiian, French, Portuguese, Italian, German, Swedish, Russian, Polish, and so forth. It's actually a somewhat rare sound in human languages. Then there's our liquid *l*. Most European languages have the two common liquids, *l* and *r*. These are easy to distinguish in German; they are easy to distinguish in Italian. They are not so easy for non-English speakers to distinguish in English. For example, pronounce the word *small* quickly, as you would in ordinary speech. A non-English speaker would find it nearly impossible to tell whether you had said *small* or *smar* or *smaw*.

There's a nice movie in which Alec Guinness, master of accents, plays a Japanese man on an ocean cruise. He says that the hardest English word for him to pronounce is *lollipop*. I'd have thought it would be *roller* or *laurel*. An acquaintance of mine who spent years attending Catholic Mass in Japan says it is our word borrowed from Hebrew, *alleluia: ah-ray-roo-rah!* Anyway, if you have only one of these liquids, it will be hard for you to hear the difference between the two, even if you play that wonderful imported American game, *besoboru*. (The only consonant that can end a Japanese word is *n,* so the Japanese had to put that extra vowel at the end of the word.) But we English speakers have nothing to crow about. In our language, we don't hear the difference between a single consonant and a doubled consonant. So when we speak Italian we make mistakes all the time. We double the consonant when it's single, and we leave it single when it ought to be doubled. We talk about an expedition to the North Chicken (*pollo* instead of *polo*), or remark that an oriole has pretty penalties (*pene* instead of *penne*), or say that the next-door neighbor has a vicious gate (*gato* instead of *gatto*).

The word *catholic* was used early on in Christian history to denote that which is believed everywhere: the whole deal. The heart of the word is Greek *holos,* meaning *whole, entire, integral.* It is not related to English *whole* or *heal.* The linking idea is that you don't want

only a part, or you don't want only to be associated with
a part. You want the whole thing. And there is only one
place to get it.

A Catholic mystic whose name I can't recall once related
a dream she had of a fallen angel. The most salient feature of said angel: no knees.

Bending the knee seems to be a gesture universally
understood in human cultures. It makes you small and
vulnerable; there's not much fighting you can do on
your knees. It may also, in a seated person, suggest
authority. So the lonely narrator in the Anglo-Saxon
elegy *The Wanderer* dreams of the days when he was
a lad, enjoying the friendship of his fellow warriors
and the good will of his kinsman and lord. He sees,
in his dream, the lord seated upon his throne, and he
approaches him, kneels, and lays his hands and then
his head upon the lord's knee, as he did in the happy
years gone by, never to come again. So Rachel, still
barren, begs Jacob to beget a child upon her serving
woman, so that when the baby is a-borning, Rachel will
take it upon her knees as her own. Even the old fash-
ioned *curtsy* that young ladies made—a compressed
and colloquial form of *courtesy*—involved a graceful
bending of the knees.

The word is pretty stable, from language to language
across the Indo-European spectrum. The Anglo-Saxon

was *cneo,* with both the *c* and the *n* pronounced: cf. German *Knie.* The Germanic c = Latin and Greek g, as Grimm tells us, and that gives us the fourth-declension Latin noun *genu, knee;* the–*gon* at the end of our words *polygon, octagon, pentagon* suggests a crook in the Greek knee, an angle. To *genuflect* is, literally, to inflect the knee, to bend the knee; it's not the same as kneeling, which we derive from Anglo-Saxon *cneowlian.* We should say *kneeled,* and did, but the analogy with *feel, felt* took over.

In fact, all our *kn* words were *cn* words in Anglo-Saxon, and were pronounced as such, as late as Chaucer (d. 1399). The good advisor to the old man in *The Merchant's Tale* warns him against taking a young thing for a wife, because, don't you know, a man can indeed hurt himself with his own *knyfe:* pronounced *knee-va,* with no silent letters. By the time of Spenser (d. 1599), the initial letter was clearly silent, or Spenser could never have written thus of his hoped-for marriage, without sounding terribly clumsy: *to knit the knot that ever shall remain.*

It's a good old Anglo-Saxon word, but it did not mean to grow angry, scowling, waiting the chance to strike. It meant, simply, *to boil.* Why didn't the Anglo-Saxons say *boil* if they meant *boil?* Or *berl,* if they were from Brooklyn-on-the-Thames? Or *bo'll,* if they were from the southern marshes? They hadn't been invaded by the French, that's why. I suppose that English stewards cooking (a French word) soup (a French word) for their dukes (a French word) would boil it—*seething* with resentment. *Boil* comes from a stock of Latin / Romance words having to do with bubbling over: an *ebullient* man is the life of the party.

The old meaning of the word *seethe* is preserved in the King James account of the manna from heaven: "Bake that which ye will bake today, and seethe that which ye will seethe" (Ex 16:23). The past tense form wasn't *seethed*, but *sod* (!): "And Jacob *sod* pottage; and Esau came from the field, and he was faint" (Gn 25:29). That didn't mean that Jacob sprinkled dirt into the stew. He *sod* the stew in a pot: he *boiled* it.

Strangely enough, we don't have the old past form, but we do still have the past participle: *sodden.* But we don't use it to mean *boiled.* Something is *sodden* when it is wet all through, usually miserably so: "I couldn't wait to take off those sodden clothes." Not boiled clothes, but *sodden,* and so almost as bad.

By the way, it does often happen that an old participle will hang on for special uses, even when it has ceased to be the regular form. It's like a black-tail suit you wear once a year for a wedding. *Sodden* is one of those. *Drunken* is another. You would not use it as the regular participle for *drink.* You would not say, "The bridegroom's mother *has drunken* a whole bottle of champagne, and is now drawing flowers on the floor with her lipstick." You would not say it, first because you are polite and don't want to call attention to somebody's new mother-in-law, but also because that's not how we use the old word *drunken*. She *has drunk* that bottle, and now is in a kind of haze: a *drunken* one.

Lent is a most unusual word. Germans call the forty-day period between Ash Wednesday and Palm Sunday by the perfectly reasonable name *Fastenzeit:* the time for fasting. The French, mishearing the Latin *quadragesima, fortieth,* call it *Carême;* whether they "hear" it as having anything to do with *quarant, forty,* well, *je ne sais pas.* The Italian *quaresima* (Italians do indeed pronounce *qu* just as we do) is closer to their *quarante, forty,* so maybe they get the connection.

But the English *Lent* has nothing to do with forty. It is our old word for springtime: when the days *lengthen.* Thus it is related to words from both the Germanic and the Romance stock: English *long,* German *lang,* Latin *longus.* Well then—why isn't it *Longth* or *Lont?* How did that *e* get in there?

And the answer is: *umlaut.* That's what happens when a vowel (German, *Laut*) turns around (German, *um*), often by the influence of a vowel in the next syllable. It's common enough. Think of the vowel in the words *cat, hat, mat.* Say those words. Now use the same vowel—say it aloud—for *carry, Harry, marry.* Tricky, ain't it? The vowel in *cat* is low: it's pronounced with the tongue low in the mouth. But the vowel *y* at the end of *carry* is high and up front: it's pronounced with the tongue near the roof of the mouth. So we anticipate the second vowel by raising the first, and instead of saying *carry, Harry, marry,* we say *Kerry, hairy, Mary.* At least, a lot of English speakers do: for them, *Larry* rhymes with *dairy.*

Some Anglo-Saxon adjectives turned into nouns by the addition of a suffix: *ith.* That eety-beety vowel in that suffix, that leetle *i,* influenced the previous vowel. It moved the *o* of *long* up front and made it *e.* Then, after it had done its dirty work, it slipped away. So we have the adjective *long,* but the noun *length;* the adjective *broad,* but the noun *breadth;* the adjective *strong,* but the noun *strength.* It couldn't do a job on the adjective *wide,* because the vowel was already high and up front (originally pronounced *weed*): *wide, width.* Avast, villain!

When I was a little boy, my grandmother got her calendar, with tear-off monthly sheets, from De Rosa's grocery store, so of course it would be a Catholic calendar, with holy days and feasts and seasons duly marked. In those days, every Friday in the year was marked with a fish, and so was Ash Wednesday. I cannot remember clearly whether *every single day in Lent* had the fish; that would make Lent the season in which the rich man and the poor man both ate what in English used to be called *Lenten fare.* How could you go all those days without meat? They didn't, exactly. That is because Sundays are not, strictly speaking, a part of Lent: there is no fast or abstinence on the joyous day of the Lord. So the rich man could eat his beef on Sunday, and the poor man could eat a bit of chicken or rabbit, if he could get it.

A Grammatical Interlude:

(just)

Some years ago I began to notice that my college freshmen had all gotten a very strange notion. They had been taught that one must never begin a sentence with the word *because*. I have no idea where high school teachers came up with this one. It is like alligators in the Manhattan sewers, or aliens landing in Roswell. Some kook huddled in a condemned building says it, and all at once everybody "knows" it, though it is not in the slightest bit true. You can imagine him with wide unblinking eyes and a frozen smile. "You must *never* begin a sentence, hee-hee, a sentence, with *because*," as he cracks walnuts with a pair of pliers.

There's nothing special about the word *because*. It's a subordinating conjunction, like a hundred others. Any of them may begin a sentence—so long as *it's a sentence they are beginning*. A sentence, whether it begins with *because* or *if* or *since* or *although* or *whenever* or *while* or *whatever* or whatever, *requires a main clause*. This is not a sentence:

Because I could not stop for death.

But it's because it lacks a main clause. Let Emily Dickinson supply one:

Because I could not stop for death, he kindly stopped for me.

The "rule" that the teachers have promulgated, besides being in itself utterly absurd, reveals something about all the other grammatical rules and "rules" that our students learn (or "learn"). That is, since grammar is no longer taught systematically, as a coherent discipline that makes sense of how we make sense, it disintegrates into a set of arbitrary directives, some of them incorrect at that, each separate from the other, without rhyme or reason. It is why I say that, unless they've studied Latin or German, *none of my college freshmen have been taught grammar.*

In any case, why would you want to begin with *because?* Well, you might want to emphasize the main clause, leaving it to the end, if that contains the idea you are going to develop. That's what Emily Dickinson wanted to do; she wanted to focus on Death's stopping by to give her a ride. Or maybe you have a lot of material that is governed by the *because,* and you don't want to string it out at the end. Instead you want it to *build toward the end,* as toward the climax. That's what John Milton did, twice over, when in *Paradise Lost* the Father declares that the Son will sit in the flesh at His right hand. I will emphasize the conjunctions in force:

Because *Thou hast, though throned in highest bliss,*
Equal to God, and equally enjoying
Godlike fruition, quitted all to save

A world from utter loss, and hast been found
By merit more than birthright Son of God,
Found worthiest to be so by being good
Far more than great or high; **because** *in Thee*
Love hath abounded more than glory abounds,
Therefore *shall thy humiliation exalt*
With Thee Thy manhood also to this throne;
Here shalt Thou sit incarnate, here shalt reign
Both God and Man, son both of God and Man,
Anointed universal King.

But maybe you want to emphasize the material in the subordinate clause. Then you will probably place it after the main clause, leaving the *because* for later:

We're off to see the Wizard,
The wonderful Wizard of Oz!
We hear he is a whiz of a wiz
If ever a wiz there was!
If ever if ever a wiz there was
The Wizard of Oz is one because
Because because because because because—
Because of the wonderful things he does!
We're off to see the Wizard,
The wonderful Wizard of Oz!

fruit

There's a word in many new Bible translations that drives me nuts. It is from one of Jesus' parables and refers to servants being sent to gather the "produce" of the land. How did that boring business-word get in there? The Greek was *karpous, fruits,* literally *things you pluck off a tree.* The Romans had their verb *carpere, to seize, to pluck,* which survives in the proverb *carpe diem, seize the day*—grab the fruit and enjoy it.

What's wrong with *produce?* Quite a lot. The linguistic register is wrong. First, Jesus is telling a parable, a story that illustrates the justice of God by means of things that anyone can see or touch. You can pick the *fruit* from a tree and load them into bushels. You can reap the ears of corn from a field, thresh it, and gather the grain into a barn. But *produce?* You log *produce* into an account book. It is an abstraction, a sort of Gross Biblical Product. Second, the elemental things of this world are in a sense closer to the mystery of God than are our human abstractions. God made the corn. God made the fruit. They are fresh from His hands. Even though we know them and see them and touch them, they are or ought to be marvels to us. They are mysterious. *Produce* is not mysterious. It is only vague. *Fruit* in its beauty may cause us to gape with wonder. *Produce* raises a yawn.

But the Latin word for *fruit, frux,* wasn't related to what you do with fruit when it's ripe. It was related to what the tree does: it *bears fruit.* In Modern English, we borrowed words directly from the Latin for the sugar that fruit contains, *fructose,* and for the virtue of stretching the fruit of your labors, *frugality,* and for making something else bear a lot of fruit, *fructify.* We had already had the word *fruit,* from the Norman French invaders; that word came from the Latin *fructus.*

Do we have any words in English that the fancy French *fruit* displaced? After all, there were fruit trees in England before the French got there, and it doesn't seem likely that the Saxons said, "Go pick me one of those things there that hang from that there tree." What does Grimm's Law say? *Never eat an apple from an ugly old lady.* Actually, as we have seen, it relates Germanic consonants to their Latin / Greek kinfolk in the Indo-European family. Grimm's Law says that Latin f = Germanic b. We are looking, then, for a Germanic word beginning with b, followed by r and a vowel (or a vowel and r; they change places a lot), followed by a back-of-the-mouth consonant. Is there such a word? Sure: Old English *byrig, mulberry:* Modern English *berry.* But that wasn't the old word for fruit in general. That old word was *aeppel:* Modern English *apple.*

That's the origin, there, of the idea in English that Adam and Eve ate an apple. What they ate was a fruit. In medieval iconography, it's usually a pear. It could have been a peach or a pear or a pomegranate—or an apple.

Conscience

In Milton's *Paradise Lost,* the Father, foreseeing the fall of man, replies to the Son's intercession by declaring that He will grant us the mercy of *conscience*:

For I will clear their senses dark,
What may suffice, and soften stony hearts,
To pray, repent, and bring obedience due.
To prayer, repentance, and obedience due,
Though but endeavored with sincere intent,
Mine ear shall not be slow, mine eye not shut.
And I will place within them as a guide
My umpire Conscience, whom if they will hear,
Light after light well-used they shall attain,
And to the end persisting, safe arrive.

What struck me for the first time about this passage, when I was presenting it to my students recently, is that little word *my*. The Father does not call conscience *an* umpire, or *the* umpire, or *their* umpire, but *my* umpire. This warrants some attention.

Conscience is literally *knowledge-with*, as if when you exercise it you place yourself as a judge over against yourself, peering into the other you's heart, or taking that tentative walk around the dim hallways and into the secret passages of the other you's motives. The excellent "translation" of the idea in Middle English was *inwit*: *into-wisdom*, *in-knowledge*, *into-seeing*. In this sense conscience does belong to us. You can't search another man's conscience; you can only assist him in searching his own, by asking careful and sensitive questions.

The other thing that makes conscience ours is that it binds us. As Cardinal Newman says, conscience has rights because it has duties. If it had no sacred duties, then we need not respect it when another man claims that it is speaking to him. Conscience is that "stern monitor" that tells us what we must do, though we would much prefer to let it go, or what we must not do, no matter how sweet it is. When it forbids or commands, it must be obeyed. No one ever tells someone, "You must disobey your conscience." Even wicked people do not do that. The temptation is always to mute the voice of the conscience, or distort it. Even wicked people shy away from openly recommending spiritual suicide.

Perhaps that explains why the Father calls the conscience *my umpire*. Conscience, it is said, is as the voice of God in man. But if that is so, then in a certain sense it is not merely private to the individual. It is *his* conscience, because it speaks to him, but it does not belong to him in the same way that his thoughts or his feelings belong to him. No doubt this voice speaks in different accents to different people and in different ages and cultures; the voice is one voice, but it is "in man" and in men, and that means its call will be understood or misunderstood in a variety of ways. What it cannot be is a mere hunch, a feeling, or, worse, a permission: that kind of roundabout way we have of talking ourselves into doing what we want to do anyway.

The *science* part of the word comes from Latin *scientia*, knowledge, built from the verb *scire, to know*. The primitive meaning seems to have been to draw distinctions: it would then be related to the root of the word *discern*; also Greek *schism, a division*, and English *shed*, whereby one thing is made to separate from another. All of which may be obscured in the word *conscience*, but is nicely brought forward by Milton's happy name for the conscience: *umpire*. "Stee-rike!" says he.

Simple Simon met a pieman,
Going to the fair;
Says Simple Simon to the pieman,
Let me taste your ware.
Says the pieman to Simple Simon,
Show me first your penny;
Says Simple Simon to the pieman,
Indeed I have not any.

Simon's a simpleton: what does that mean? He can add and subtract, but can't do long division? Off to the American college goes he!

Finding the word's immediate origin is simple enough: French *simple,* from Latin *simplex* (Italian *semplice*). But the Latin word is fascinating. It's a combination of two parts, the *sim* and the *plex*. The *sim* implies *one,* as in *only one:* cf. *single.* The *plex* is related to a group of words having to do with weaving or knotting or wrapping. Something that is *complex* is full of tangles: a knotty problem, we say. A person who is *duplicitous* has one face and shows another. He's two-ply. For bathroom tissue, that's good, but not so for people. Hence we have the Latin name *Simplicius,* and its augmented *Simplicianus.* One fine and patient Christian by that name figures in Augustine's *Confessions.* He is the friend of the famous orator Victorinus, who for years kept assuring Simplicianus that he was really a Christian inside. Well, you can't testify to Christ "inside," because if you keep your testimony to yourself, you aren't testifying at all. We remember Christ's warning to us, not to deny Him before men, lest He deny us before the Father. Simplicianus replied to him always, "I will not believe it until I see you baptized." Eventually Victorinus came round, drawing near to the end of his life, and therefore near to the time when there will be "no shuffling," as the guilty king in *Hamlet* admits: when we ourselves will be

> *compelled,*
> *Even to the teeth and forehead of our faults,*
> *To give in evidence.*

So one day he said at last, "I want to be a Christian," bringing joy to the heart of his frank and honest friend.

Are there any fine old English words in the fold? Yes, there are. Words in Latin that begin with *p* correspond with Germanic words beginning with *f:* and the word we're looking for here will also have an *l* in it: *fold.* Something made *manifold* has been *multiplied;* the words are mirrors of one another. Something *twofold* is *duplex,* or, through French, *doubled.*

So a *simple* person has only one side. What you see is what you get. If only politicians were so. Then they would be more like God Himself. That would come as news to one of my students, who recently wrote that God was too *complex* a being for man to understand. Of course the reverse is true. The universe is *complex,* literally *folded in upon itself,* because it is made up of many parts. A rose petal is *complex.* God is unfathomable not because He is *complex,* but because He is *simplicity itself, unity,* the One who is, without qualification, without parts, without change: the center and circumference of all things.

That *perplexes* us, because we have no direct experience of such simplicity. For us, everything that we learn, unless it is given to us in a simple flash of insight, is a tangled knot to untie. It is a *perplexity,* something all folded and wrapped up and interwoven: Latin *per-* suggests something done to the bitter end, through and through, sometimes through and back and through and back, sometimes wrong way out. Hence someone is *per-turbed,* literally roiling with *crowds thronging hither and thither.*

I'm quite aware that this word, in Massachusetts and New York, seems to mean, at least on traffic signs,

"Speed up and get in front of the guy who has the right of way!" Interstate highways aside, though, it's a nice word. It has come to mean *to give way,* as when a corrupt Claude Rains is trying to shout down Jimmy Stewart in the halls of Congress: "Will the gentleman yield!" "No, I w-won't yield!" And the hearts of Boy Scouts leap (*Mr. Smith Goes to Washington*).

Its original meaning, though, suggests generosity, bounty, fruitfulness. Recipes in women's magazines used to conclude with the *yield:* two dozen cupcakes, as the case might be. Farmers still discuss what their harvests will *yield* per acre. The word comes from a good Anglo-Saxon verb, *gieldan,* meaning *to yield, to produce, to be worth.* Its root is the same that gives us German *Geld, money.* We pronounce it with a *y,* because of the effect of the high front vowel after the *g: g's* are notoriously unstable. For example, Latin *g* before the front vowels *e* and *i* became the sound *dzh* in Italian (as in English *general*), *zh* in French (as in English *corsage*), and a hard *h* in Spanish (as in English *junta*). This explains plenty of *g-y* doublets in Germanic languages, whereby a word split into two when a change in pronunciation occurred in one area but not in another: *yard, garden.*

Now, ol' *gieldan* was a Strong Verb. It's since lost its strength; now it just sighs and takes the drab past tense that all the other weaklings take: *yielded.* But in the old days it wasn't so. In the old days, *gieldan* marched proudly into the sunset, with all its principal parts a-shining: *gieldan, geald, guldon, golden.* See? The last two of those had back-of-the-mouth vowels following the *g,* so the change to the *y*-sound never happened. Suggestive, aren't they, those last two? I know what you're thinking. "Then *yield* is related to *gold,* maybe?"

Yes, it is. Those words are cousins, along with *yellow* (German *gelb*), for reasons you can guess.

Meanwhile, the Anglo-Saxons took the noun *gold* and made a verb out of it, by adding the causative suffix *-jan,* which raised the preceding vowel and resulted in a new verb, *gyldan,* meaning to make something gold: Modern English *gild.* We're glad they did this, or we'd never have had this piece of poetry, care of the cartoonist Chuck Jones:

> *I'm a tweet widdo bird in a dilded cayds,*
> *Tweety's my name but I don't know my ayds!*

We also would never have had the scornful name for the late nineteenth century in America: *The Gilded Age.* That was when writers like Mark Twain and William Dean Howells suggested that the virtues of the newly rich industrialists were like *gilt* on wood or plaster: glittery and thinner than paper. If that was the Gilded Age, what is ours? We might hire for the job a sick cousin of *gold* and *gild:* The *Jaundiced* Age, yellow with the bile of a dying liver.

> *And peace will guide the planets,*
> *And love will steer the stars!*
> *This is the Age of Aquarius, the Age of Aquarius,*
> *Aquarius, Aquarius!*
> *(The Age of Aquarius,* Rado, Ragni, MacDermot)

The hit song with the catchy, gimmicky tune and the inane lyrics was written for the musical *Hair,* in which the singing actors stripped to the altogether and showed more hair than decent people cared to see. It's astonishing to consider how quickly not only moral sensibility but *taste* collapsed, so that people soon were doing in public what would have roused disdain and ridicule only a few years before. *Hair* hit the stage in 1969. If you watch a tape of Game One of the 1968 World Series between the Cardinals and the Tigers, you'll notice that the women are wearing dresses and hats, and the men are wearing white button-down shirts. That was in early October, in St. Louis, on a very hot and muggy day. Bob Gibson struck out seventeen men in that game (still a World Series record), shutting the Tigers out, 4–0. You can tell how hot it was by the sweat pouring from his forehead and cheeks. And yet the people were well dressed. By 1975, you'd see shirtless men with painted bellies, and baseball would have a big problem with drunks in the crowd.

The Age of Aquarius was supposed to be dawning, bringing about Peace on Earth. How was that to happen? Well, everybody was supposed to be too busy mounting one another or being mounted; making love and not war. Any decent pagan philosopher, not to mention the millennia of wisdom from the Jewish and Christian Scriptures and their interpreters, could have told them about the essential cruelty of lust, but nobody was listening. We still have wars, quite a lot of them, but we also enjoy the delight of destroyed communities and families; morally and socially, we live among the bombed-out ruins of what once was a great and good nation. And we don't even derive the "benefits" of eros.

C. S. Lewis could have predicted that, too. Eros is a cruel master. People who submit themselves to eros as if it were the greatest of human aims soon find that they lose not only the greater goods but eros itself, as they must go farther afield and strive with redoubled energy to muster the excitement that once accompanied their first violations of the moral law. Call it the Age of the Desert. What's the astrological sign for loneliness, divorce, dead babies, and the boredom of squalor?

"Peace," said Saint Augustine, "is the tranquility of order." That is about as brilliant a sentence as has ever been written, connecting in a subtle and suggestive way three states of being, each having to do with the others. He does not say that it is the mere absence of war, or the dull blank of inactivity, or the settling of ruffled nerves. *Peace* is like the play of a gentle breeze upon clear waters, or the twinkle in the eye of your spouse as you sit on the porch watching the children at their games. All is right, all is well. In this peace there is a fullness of life; it is what Max Picard says we enjoy in the World of Silence.

Words for this tranquility of order are rich in their various associations. Our word *peace* comes from the Norman French, and ultimately from Latin *pax*. Its original sense was of a *pact*, something that you and your neighbor made fast, perhaps with a hearty handshake: cf. German *fangen, to seize.* "Peace I leave you, my peace I give you," said the risen Jesus to the apostles, and those words are echoed in the Catholic Mass just before communion, in what used to be called, simply, the *Pax*. I like very much its use in the silver dollar minted just after World War I: the Peace Dollar. Miss Liberty on the obverse is a young woman whose hair streams in the wind. Her lips are parted, as if she were speaking the word that man must hear. On the reverse is the usual bald eagle, but not in flight. He is perched on a rock, upon which we read the inscription, unique in American coinage: PEACE.

For my money the most excellent word for peace is the Hebrew *shalom*. What does it mean? What does it not mean? It suggests peace after war, wholeness, health, agreement, the light of a friendly countenance. If it were translated literally every time it appears in the Old Testament, we would find peace winking at us from everywhere. Young men go for war. I'm not young anymore. I long for peace, the tranquility of order.

Lily Munster walks about the tumbledown parlor, shaking a mop-like thing over the pump organ, the raven-clock, the sofa, and the electric chair. Smoke scatters everywhere. "Excuse me," she says to the astonished visitor, "I was just *dusting* the furniture."

The joke's on us English speakers. How odd it is, that we turn nouns into verbs, just like that, to mean that we put that noun *onto* something else. We paint things by putting paint on them. We soil things by smudging them with soil. We nail things by driving nails into them. We water flowers. And yes, Lily, we *dust crops!*

What's odder still is that we have a group of verbs, many of them having to do with preparing plants or animals for our tables, which mean that we take the noun *away* from something. Olives that are *pitted* have no pits. Cherries that are *stoned,* if they are not on college campuses, have no stones. You *shell* peas by taking them out of their shells. The kid on roller skates hits a bump in the sidewalk and *skins* his knees. It means that his knees had skin on them, and don't anymore. "Gimme that wrench or I'll *brain* ya!" says Moe to Curly. It is not clear in Curly's case whether such an operation could be performed, but we know what Moe means.

Many of the other verbs are common enough, and even when they're not so common we understand them readily, by analogy: *peel, hull, shuck, husk, bone, scalp, juice.* If you *bark your shins* against a rock, you've stripped the flesh off just as if you'd barked a tree to prepare it for planing. A fire *guts* a house: it burns the guts of it right out. One of these verbs is now common but entirely figurative: *sap.* It means *to take away all the strength* from something, slowly but inexorably. But its original meaning is just as it says: to drain the sap away. Thomas Jefferson feared that the Supreme Court would act as *sappers,* slowly and silently draining away the liberties of the people. Where on earth could he have gotten such a notion?

All my life long, feminists have claimed that language used to describe women was either nasty or condescending or narrow-minded. I don't intend here to placate them. You can't cool a volcano with an ice cube. I simply mean to show how language can turn an ordinary word into a term of high honor; and can do the reverse, applying a term of high honor to ordinary people.

I have in mind that fine old word that names Lucy Van Pelt's dearest ambition: *queen.* It's an Old English word, *cwen,* and designates royalty. What's odd is that the word was lost by the typically more conservative German language. In German, the man with the crown on his head is *der Koenig* (Old English *cyning,* the *c* pronounced like *k*; Modern English *king*). But the woman with the crown on her head is the king-with-feminine-suffix: *die Koenigin* (cf. Modern English *actor, actress; steward, stewardess*). But the Scandinavians retained the word, and here's the interesting thing. In the back of a Swedish restaurant you'll see two doors. One of them will read *kvinnar:* women. In Sweden, that's just the word for woman: *kvinna.* In our time, of course, it may be a matter of controversy. Our grandparents would wonder about the sex of a child before it was born. They didn't have ultrasounds. We are the first generation of human beings who wonder about the sex of a child *after* it is born. We do have ultrasounds. It's brains we lack.

Which came first, the ordinary or the honorary? In this case, probably the ordinary. Grimm's Law instructs us to look for Greek or Latin *g* when we find Germanic *c* (*k*), and sure enough, Greek *gyne* corresponds exactly with Old English *cwen* (the Scandinavians turned the *w* into a *v*, or we'd be calling the football team the Minnesota *Wikings*). But there is a dusty old word in English that seems to have gone down the other track, all the way down, and then fallen into a linguistic slum: *quean,* meaning *harlot.* Mary *Quean of Scots?* I don't know.

bewildered

Have you ever been sauntering in the woods and taken an odd turn, and found yourself always on the wrong side of a lake or a stream, or expecting the next hilltop to clear everything up, but when you reach it you don't recognize anything? And then the sun hides behind a wall of iron gray clouds and you can no longer tell where the south is, and you expect that if you keep walking in one direction you'll inevitably come upon a certain highway. But the highway turns out to be a deer path. You're quite confused and you don't know where to turn. You are *bewildered:* literally, you are lost in a wilderness.

It's a funny word, *bewilder,* dependent for its force upon the causative prefix *be-.* In many English words, that causative sense is obscured by our no longer recognizing the meaning of the root. It's hard for us to see what the *be-* means in *bequeath,* because we don't know what it means to *queath;* but the sense becomes clear if we are told that Old English *cwethan* means to speak (cf. the archaic form *quoth,* from the past tense *cwaeth*). So to *bequeath* is to *bespeak,* that is, to promise somebody something; now, to promise to a beneficiary something in your will. In some other words, ones that we readily recognize, the causative implies an intensification: it's one thing to be *spattered* with blood, but to be *bespattered* with it is to be in a fine mess indeed.

But we do have several words with the causative prefix, which involve some distressing or incapacitating condition named in the root. These are analogous to *bewilder,* and, like *bewilder,* have sometimes lost their most specific sense. So, to be *benighted* means to suffer the distress of darkness, literally, to be lost somewhere in the middle of the night. That participle has long been applied to the *opinions* of people we don't like. You are *benighted,* perhaps, if you think that the latest political craze is as valuable as a new brand of soap. If you are *becalmed* at sea, you are stuck in the middle of the ocean with no wind to fill your sails. If you are *bedazzled,* you are quite lost in an excess of light; you are so blinded, so dazzled and dazed, you cannot tell where you are.

What about *befuddled?* Does it mean that you're full of *fuddle?* Yes, actually, it does. To *fuddle* was to get drunk. Someone who is *befuddled* is all confused, and that is why he meant to dial his insurance company but dialed the police instead.

Sometimes we can tell things about a nation's climate or a people's way of life by the words they have, or don't have. There were apples in England in the time of Bede the Venerable, in the eighth century. But there were no peaches. That word enters the English language only after the Norman invasion. The French brought their ships full of words with them, and along with those words they brought things to eat and drink, among which must have been the worthy peach: French *pêche.* The little "hat" over the vowel in *pêche* marks where an *s* used to be. Why the French cared to mark a consonant they no longer pronounced, I don't know, but there it is.

The hat gives us a clue that the French word is the same as the Italian *persica, peach* (cf. German *Pfirsich*). The word literally means *the Persian thing.* The peach wasn't native to western Europe, but was brought back west by Roman traders with the Persians, who lived in modern day Iran. Indeed, it wasn't that long ago when westerners referred to that whole area as Persia. The ancient Greeks did a lot of wrangling and trading, fighting and allying, with those Persians, so there are words we take for granted as "western" that really come from Persia: *paradise,* for example. Iran wasn't then a hot and cold desert for maniacal mullahs, but a heady land of grain and fruit and hedonistic pleasures and despots and slaves. The Greeks called them *barbaroi* because their language sounded like *ba-ba-ba-ba-babble;* the word came to mean *people who don't have the good fortune of living the lives of free men, like Greeks.* And yet, the Persian language is in the stable with other Indo-European languages; it is *not* a Semitic tongue; it is not related to Hebrew and Arabic. It is related to Greek, though the Greeks probably didn't know it.

There are peaches in New Jersey, so I don't see why there should not have been peaches in Paradise. That

Persian word borrowed into Greek and Latin and then into our modern languages suggests an enclosure: an intimate garden with a wall about it. Milton understood the point, and made the garden in his Eden a kind of elevated area the size of Rhode Island, bounded with natural "walls" of earth and trees, and giving Adam a fine and royal prospect from which to look out upon the world beyond. The idea is also present when the masters painted the Annunciation, placing Mary and the angel Gabriel within a paradise: "A garden enclosed is my beloved," says the bridegroom in the Song of Songs (see 4:12).

Along with the fruit and the spices and the name of Paradise, a fascinating game came west from Persia, named for the crucial piece in it, the king. The Persian word for king is *shah,* as in the Shah of Iran. The word underwent various transformations before it became English *chess,* but its Persian origin can be divined very clearly by the German form of the word: *Schach.*

Let's suppose you are inventing your own language. You have an ordinary verb, say, *drink,* and you want to turn it into a verb that means "make somebody else drink," or, with gritty resolution, "make darned sure that somebody else has drunk!" You don't want to use a phrase. You don't even want to use a suffix if you don't have to. Just a tiny change in the verb, to make it *causative:* that's what you want.

And that's what those linguistic sophisticates, the early Germans, had. They marked causation by a little semivowel insertion into the verb: our old friend the hard *y*, spelled *j*. But there was a twist to the insertion. They didn't use the present tense. They used the *past tense*. That makes sense; the cause isn't really a cause unless it has completed the action already.

We see this in the good old verb *drink:* Old English *drincan*. That was a strong verb—with muscles like cords, able to form its own past tense and past participle: *drincan, dranc, druncon, druncen*. It's in a class of strong Germanic verbs that follow the pattern i-a-u: *sing, sang, sung; stink, stank, stunk; spin, *span, spun; sling, *slang, slung; sink, sank, sunk; swim, swam, swum* (you can find in the King James Bible the forms I've marked with an asterisk). Anyhow, we take the past form *dranc*, and form the new verb **drancjan*. Over time, the influence of the following hard *y* sound, made at the top of the mouth, raised the vowel in the previous syllable, from *a* to *e;* and the *j* dropped out: *drencan*. There's our verb: *drench, to soak somebody*.

doom

"Oh no! I said, *if* the Great Pumpkin appears!" says Linus, his hands over his lips. "I'm *doomed!*" We hear something of that foreboding in these lines from Shakespeare's great paean to the immutability of love:

Love's not Time's fool, though rosy lips and
  cheeks
Within his bending sickle's compass come;
Love alters not with his spare hours and weeks
But bears it out unto the edge of doom.

Linus means that he's in for an unfortunate destiny.
Shakespeare means something a little different, something denoted by that extraordinarily suggestive phrase
from Scripture, *the trump of doom.* The word means
judgment; and *the edge of doom* takes us to the terrible break of dawn on Judgment Day—in Anglo-Saxon,
domes daeg, our *day of doom, Doomsday.*

The word in Anglo-Saxon simply meant *judgment,*
of the rightness or wrongness of a course of action,
which could be wise or foolhardy; or of the good or evil
of a man. It is a cousin of the Greek *themis,* the ancient
word to suggest a wise and fundamental righteousness,
a proper order in man and the world around us. It was
strictly a noun; you couldn't *doom* somebody in Anglo-
Saxon, at least not with that word. They did, however,
make a causative verb out of it: **domjan, to make a
judgment.* The *j* pushed the previous vowel to the front
(the umlaut we have met before), and then dropped
away, so that **domjan* became *deman: deem.* To *deem*
is to make a *doom:* it is to judge. A man who rode the
circuits as a judge was a *dem-ster:* the common modern
surname *Dempster.*

It's interesting, though, to consider that the word
has attracted a sense that the judgment is probably
going to be a fearful one. Perhaps that's our guilty con-
sciences speaking honestly for once. Hence we get the
half-mocking but half-nervous rhyming doublet, *doom*

and gloom. That's appropriate, because what happened to *doom* also happened to *gloom.* It used to denote a glimmering light, such as at sunset—*in the gloaming,* as the old song puts it. Now that soft light of evening is shrouded in darkness. Funny how that happened to that word, but not to its kinfolk, *glee, gleam, glisten, glitter, glow.*

Beside the word *nescient* in Dr. E's Imaginary Dictionary stands an illustration of a bureaucrat, smug and smiling benignantly upon an ordinary citizen. The cross-reference reads: See *Expert.* The word means what you'd guess: *the property of knowing absolutely nothing.* In Latin, someone in that state, let's say a simpleton or a senator, is *nescius: not presciens,* which means that you know things beforehand, or *omnisciens,* which means that you know everything, or *consciens,* which means that you grasp something profound about yourself and the world around you, but *nescius: non-knowing.*

That word, through Old French, entered English as *nice,* meaning *stupid, silly, ignorant, foolish.* It was not a very nice word. But then it underwent a transformation. By the time of Spenser and Shakespeare, it had come to acquire the ambivalent sense of a usually foolish preciseness, as in our word *niceties,* generally suggesting an annoying emphasis on the trivial.

In this regard it seems to have walked the same track as the word *dainty*, which Spenser usually employs to refer to something delicately beautiful, but sometimes to refer to people who are fussy or persnickety or unwholesomely preoccupied with cleanliness. But *nice*, in Spenser, is always an insult: *nice* hands will not get themselves bloody to help a dying man. When Milton wants to describe all the lush growing greenery in Paradise, he says pointedly that niceness is the last thing we want. No, God gives us

> *flowers which not nice Art*
> *In beds and curious knots, but Nature boon*
> *Poured forth profuse in hill and dale and plain.*

The association with unreasonable fussiness gradually changed, so that someone with keen insight can make a *nice distinction;* if at first that meant a distinction without a difference, made by a fool, it now means a fine distinction that makes a big difference, which only a wise person can make. Taking the word in another direction, though, the ladies began to use it to refer to something decorated in a pleasantly fussy way: a nice hat, a nice ribbon. From thence it has come to denote kindness generally, "He's a nice man," but with the *possibility* of hollowness and triviality lurking around the corner.

C. S. Lewis understood the word quite well, which is why, in *That Hideous Strength,* the N. I. C. E. (National Institute of Coordinated Experiments) is England's metastatic locus of evil. For, as Lewis says, the angels do not bow before the Lord, singing, "Nice, nice, nice," but "Holy, holy, holy!"

posse

That's what the men of Dry Gulch do in the westerns, when the marshal sets out to find the horse thieves and bring them to justice. They form the legally sanctioned body of citizens known as a *posse comitatus*, from the Latin words granting the authorities that permission: *posse* is simply the Latin infinitive meaning *to be able, to have the power*. It's a contraction of **potesse*, its first part related to all kinds of English words having to do with ability: *potential, power* (through Old French), *potentate, possible*.

It shouldn't surprise us that people in isolated places preserve more of the old linguistic forms than do people in urban centers. There's simply more roiling and boiling in the cities; and, in sparsely populated areas, higher costs attendant upon misunderstanding. The funny thing is, though, that city dwellers look down upon the speech of the hillbillies as if it were rough and dimwitted, when actually the speech of those same hill-billies more nearly resembles that of Shakespeare than does the speech of the city dwellers.

Take these words from the common vocabulary of Jed Clampett of happy memory: *varmint, vittles, reckon, a-fixing*. The first, *varmint*, is just the old word *vermin* (cf. Latin *vermus, worm*) referring not to mice but to inconvenient animals generally, pro-nounced with the typical British turn of *-er* to *-ar*, giving us the surnames *Darby (Derby)* and *Clark (Clerk)*; to this day the English Queen will mention the "clark" at the drug store, not the "clurk." The word *victuals* is straight out of Renaissance English: the man who sells food provisions is a *victualer*, pronounced *vitt-el-er*; the transformation of *-tu-* to *-ch-* had not been completed by Shakespeare's time, nor that of *-ti-* to *-sh-* in words like *nation* (sometimes trisyllabic in Shakespeare and his contemporaries, but never so in Milton: *na-see-on, na-tsee-on, na-shee-on*). Shakespeare probably pronounced *creature* not like our *creecher*, but something like *cray-tyoor*, closer to Jed's *critter*. The word *reckon* for *think* continues the ancient association of judgment with numbers. "That doesn't tally," we say, meaning that the reasoning isn't right; or, "I can't tell," meaning "I can't account for it" (cf. English *teller*, the person at the bank who *counts* your money). Then there's *a-fixing*. The prefix *a-*, to denote that an action is ongoing, in the process, is as old as English itself: it is an unstressed shortening of the prefixed preposition *on-*, as in, well, *ongoing*. It is quite useful, particularly to denote a *passive sense*: "Lookie, Rafe, that house has been a-building nigh unto three year!" Believe it or not, (head nod to Mr. Ripley): *Everything in that sentence that strikes us as incorrect or low is of venerable age.*

As it is good to remember. There is no reason why we should deprive ourselves of the richness of the old and venerable. "Hallowed be Thy name," we pray, and if that strikes some as too "high," they should trouble to become acquainted with the poetic Hebrew of the psalms, wherein many an old word or form appears that you would not use while you were dickering with your neighbor over the price of a lamb. Bureaucrats may not understand it, but why should we pray like bureaucrats? "Memo to God: Send help." Really?

I saw Eternity the other night,
Like a great ring of pure and endless light,
All calm, as it was bright;
And round beneath it, Time in hours, days,
*   years,*
Driven by the spheres
Like a vast shadow moved; in which the world
And all her train were hurled.
                    —*from* The World, *Herbert Vaughan*

My students have a habit, when they are discussing theological writings about what Italians expressively call the *al di là*—the Over Yonder, of calling eternal life the *afterlife*. I confess that I can't stand the word. It reminds me of an afterthought or an afterword or an aftertaste, as if this life were a dish of garlic and cucumbers, and what comes after is the heavenly eructation. I do not believe that Saint Jerome had that in mind when he translated the opening words of the joyful psalm, *Eructavit cor meum verbum bonum: My heart has uttered a good word.* Let monks burping at supper in a refectory make the jest.

Anyway, the word *afterlife* seems to get things exactly backwards. C. S. Lewis is right to say that for the

Christian, these here are the shadowlands, and this life now is a kind of preface before the first chapter, before life really begins. This is the prelude; life in the presence of God is the symphony. Or maybe it is not even the prelude. It is the time when the musicians tune their instruments and the singers clear their throats and the conductor cracks his knuckles. Jesus does not say to the repentant thief, "This day you will enter the afterlife." He says, "This day you shall be with me in Paradise." Saint Paul does not say to the Corinthians that death stings a little, but then you go on lingering as in a never-ending coda. He says that what is sown a corruptible body rises an incorruptible body. It is to stuff the mouth of death with death, and bring into being something that is not simply a continuation of what went before. "Behold," says the One seated on the throne, "I make all things new."

So Christians talk not about an *afterlife* but about a new life, *eternal* life, life outside of time as we now experience it. Time does not measure God, since God is the maker of time. When I first read about that in the latter books of Augustine's *Confessions*, it was as if a key turned in a lock, and a door opened, and everything became clear. The whole universe, even supposing that it always existed and always would exist, would still be but a creature, and therefore circumscribed. It need not have been as it is. It might be perpetual, but it would not be *eternal*. The old Thomist and friend of the Maritains, Pere Garrigou-Lagrange, uses the term *aeviternal* to describe the angels, created incorporeal and immortal. Lewis uses the Latin *longaevi, long-aged,* to describe the long-living creatures of European folklore, such as the elves.

Both of those words are still related to our word *eternal*. That word is made up of two main parts: the *-ternal*, which is just a suffix, and the root, *e*. That root is not the prefix *e-*, a reduction of the preposition *ex* before certain consonants: *e-ject, to throw out*; *e-rode, to gnaw away*; *e-mit, to send forth*. The *e* in *eternal* comes from a very active Indo-European root that suggests the force of life, robust and enduring. It is the source of Latin *aevum, age, era*, which is itself the foundation stone for *aeviternus*, then reduced to *aeternus, beyond the ages*. The *e* is also to be found in Greek *aion*, borrowed into English as *eon*, and that's the word in the New Testament that is rendered as *forever and ever*, in the phrase *aion aionon*.

nincompoop

Some of our funniest English words come from the mangling of foreign words, often Latin. A *nincompoop* is *non compos mentis: not capable in the mind*. Here the mangled word has a considerable advantage over the precise Latin: *nincompoop* sounds like something that fits a *nincompoop*. There's a blasphemous example of such mangling in our *hocus-pocus:* it's from the Latin said at the consecration of the bread during Mass, when the priest says, *Hoc est enim corpus meum, For this is My body*. Say "hoc est corpus" very fast, twenty times, and you'll hear how we got it.

"Let's *vamoose,*" says Grandpa to the boy, as they start to pack up their fishing tackle. Grandpa is just using the scrunched form of Spanish *vamanos, let's go,* heard over and over by ranchers and cowboys in the southwest. The lady relaxes in the backyard on what she and everybody else now pronounces as a "shays lounge," thinking that the thing is for lounging, when actually the French phrase is *chaise longue, a long chair.*

Soldiers and sailors are great sources of foreign words, turned sort-of-English. Take the word *savvy:* no word in English rhymes with it, and only the coined word *flivver* (for a cheap car or plane) looks like it. It's from French *savoir, to know*, or perhaps Spanish *sabe*; the men used it to mean *know-how, shrewdness.* That's of relatively recent entry into English. Much older is the quasi-military word *parley,* straight from French *parler, to speak:* it describes what happens when opposing armies call a truce and come together to talk. Many of our nautical words come from the Dutch—for a century at least they had the greatest navy in the world. The most obvious of such words is *boom,* the Dutch word for *tree* (cf. German *Baum,* English *beam = plank*). That's what it means to *lower the boom:* to lower the enormous tree affixed to the mast. It has nothing to do with a loud noise—unless the boom hits the deck.

When the immensely inventive writers during the Renaissance searched for words, they often got them right from Latin and made them English for their purposes. This means that there are thousands of words in English, and very common words among them, which are closer to the original Latin than their counterparts in the Romance languages are.

The trick is to remember what those words really mean, especially when you're reading poetry. So, for instance, when we *exclude* somebody, we literally shut the door on them; when we *insinuate,* we literally sneak our way into someone's bosom; and when we *protect* someone, we put up a roof before him for shelter (cf. Latin *tectum, roof;* Italian *tetto*). When we *detect* something, we pull the roof off it, for all the world to see.

The *tec-* part of the word has quite a few kinsmen all over the Indo-European map, as we might expect for so common and necessary a thing as a roof. If we put it through Grimm's Wringer, we see the word growing more specific and concrete. Grimm instructs us to see Germanic *th* as the equivalent of Latin *t:* and sure enough we have the Anglo-Saxon *theccan* (pronounced *thetch-chan*), to *thatch* (cf. German *Dach, roof*). Well, why not? That's how people made their roofs. This was especially so the farther north you went. In fact, in mud-rich and hardwood-poor Ireland and Scotland, you might make your whole house out of the stuff:

> *I shall arise and go now, and go to Innisfree,*
> *And a small cabin build there, of clay and wat-*
> *tles made.*

So the word for *roof* in southern climes is the word for *house* among the Celts that moved north: Welsh *ty,* Irish *taigh,* Gaelic *tigh* (pronounced *tee*). Anybody out

there with the surname *Tighe?* But in Italy and Greece
you didn't have to use sod and mud. You could use clay,
rounded into shapes that would shed the rainwater. So
you roofed your house with *teguli:* English *tiles.*

The most powerful instance of a roof in Scripture
was obscured in our English Mass for nearly forty years,
the work of bad translators who reacted to poetry the
way some people react to ragweed. "Lord, I am not worthy to receive you," we said before communion. That
was not right. Let us remember the scene. The centurion in the Gospels has a beloved servant who is suffering acutely and is near death. He sends for Jesus.
When Jesus replies that He will go to the man's house,
the centurion—a friend of the Jews, though a pagan,
and possibly a man who has been half-converted to the
Jewish faith—says, "Lord, I am not worthy that thou
shouldst enter under my roof," (Greek *stege,* with a
variant *tege,* related to all of those words above) "but
only say the word and my servant shall be healed."
The centurion sees in his mind's eye the Lord entering under the protection of his roof, as if *he* were lord
over Jesus. Sensitive to right order, he demurs. "I have
not found such great faith in all of Israel," says Jesus in
astonishment (Mt 8:8–10).

It may come as a surprise, but some of our most common words are of unknown origin. That is the case

with both *boy* and *girl*. The former suddenly appears
in Middle English, with the latter first denoting a small
child of either sex. For a while, the word *child* in some
dialects traded places with the word *girl*, so that the
shepherd in Shakespeare's *The Winter's Tale*, finding
a foundling baby, asks himself whether it is a boy or a
child. But pretty soon the words came to assume our
familiar meanings.

What's interesting about the word *boy*, though, are
the secondary associations, and the parallels with these
in other languages. Feminists complain about the word
girl, but except for the use of the word on the seamy
side of the street—*call girls, saloon girls*—the word
generally suggests youth, beauty, and amiability. It's
boy that's all over the map. It could be a term of condescending endearment. "In, boy, go first," says King
Lear to the Fool, when the storm is raging on the heath,
and the hovel stands near for a most poor shelter. It's a
moment of telling humility in the old man, who is not
known for such. We don't know how old the Fool is. He
is probably not very old, but he seems to be a man well
past his boyhood.

The word *boy*, then, suggests a servant; a *houseboy*
could be taking aspirin for arthritis. When the centurion asked Jesus to heal his beloved servant, the word
in Greek is *pais, boy* (cf. English *pedagogue, someone who teaches boys*). Saint Jerome translated it by
the Latin *puer, boy*. Many white men in the American
South, in decades past, would address a black man as
boy, without regard to age. The word there was not at
all affectionate, but was meant to stress the black man's
inferior social status, even his servitude. German *Knabe*
followed along the same track: it originally referred to a

servant, and came to refer to a boy, while in English it soured from servility to villainy: *knave*. Spenser, in the late sixteenth century, uses *boy* to refer to grown men who are fools. The word is marked not only for youth but inadequacy: *Never send a boy to do a man's job.*

And yet—men who speak English use the word all the time to refer to one another, as comrades, teammates, close friends: "Let's go, boys!" Every man cherishes being *one of the boys*; and this masculine delight in boyishness crosses every linguistic border I know of. "*Vamanos, muchachos!*" they say in Mexico—*let's go, boys*! And in Italian: "*Andiamo, ragazzi!*" And in German: "*Gehen wir, Jungens!*" And in Latin: "*Venite, juvenes!*" See that old man deck the drunk and toss him out on his backside? Attaboy!

Our word is two thousand years old, and, other than undergoing the Great Vowel Shift (which naughty linguists call the Great Vowel Movement; please file this jest under "The Lonely Lives of Philologists"), has remained just as it was. But it's a profound word for a profound idea. A computer is not wise, no more than a file cabinet or a dictionary is wise. A man who can spout one bit of data after another may be a complete fool. Data are not information (because they possess no form), information is not knowledge (because knowledge implies understanding), and knowledge is not wisdom (because wisdom implies insight into the nature of man and the world). A datum is impersonal and atomized. Information possesses structure but is impersonal. Knowledge is personal but not necessarily universal or moral or spiritual. Wisdom is *necessarily* personal, universal, and moral.

The etymology of the word suggests why. The *wise* man is literally the one who *sees*. The word is related to the Anglo-Saxon word *witan, to understand:* Modern German *wissen, to know*. From that word we derive our *wit*, which has degenerated into a term denoting a quick humor, or a quick perception of things going on nearby, especially if they require instant decision: then you must have your *wits* about you. When I was a small boy I couldn't fathom what those *wits* were supposed to be; I thought vaguely that they had something to do with your waist. In Shakespeare's time, to be *witty* might be downright sinister, as when Richard III, newly crowned, begins to suspect the aims of the man who put him on the throne, "the deep revolving *witty* Buckingham." But it's the Latin and Greek cousins that reveal the essence of this word. The ancient Romans had the *w* consonant, which they spelled as *v;* Grimm's Law also tells us that we should heed old men with long white beards, and that Germanic *t* = Roman *d*. So then, Germanic *wit-* corresponds to Latin *vid-,* as in the important verb *videre: to see*. So a wise man is *prudent, seeing forward* (Latin *providens*); he can see to things and give advice (Latin *advisus*); he is a man of vision (Latin *visio*).

The Greeks didn't have that initial *w,* or at least not in the place and time when the great classical authors were writing. What remains of that consonant is preserved, though, in the diphthong in *oid-,* the root of Greek verbs having to do with vision. Our most important word from that barrel: *idea:* literally, *a picture in the mind,* something you see; recall the cartoon lightbulbs shining over the head of somebody who suddenly sees the thing to do. William Golding was on to this in his eerie novel *The Inheritors,* about a dire encounter between innocent but dim Neanderthals and our farther-seeing and cruel ancestors. When a small family knot of Neanderthals is confronted with a deep rushing stream, they back away in fear, but the sharpest among them, seeing a big tree limb nearby, cries out, "I have a picture!" And he shows them how to cross the stream. He had an *idea.*

In the Hebrew tradition, the wise man isn't the one who can perform feats of sophisticated calculation, but rather he to whom God has granted vision. So the psalmist's longing to behold the face of God is also at once a longing for wisdom; *to see,* in the deepest sense of the word. For now, we see as in a glass, darkly; but then, face-to-face (see 1 Cor 13:12).

That wasn't what the acerbic philosopher Diogenes called himself. You may remember him: the fellow who wandered about the streets with a lantern, saying that he was looking for one honest man. He also made a habit of relieving himself in public. Alexander the Great, that half-barbarian emperor who hankered after

sophisticated ways, once stood over Diogenes as he
was sitting on the ground. Alexander asked Diogenes if
he could do anything for him, and Diogenes said yes, he
could. He could get out of his light.

The Greeks found Diogenes and his fellows really
unpleasant, so they called them the dog-philosophers,
cynicoi, from *cynoi, dogs.* Man's best friend isn't always
viewed as such in ancient literature. The Romans loved
dogs, and Odysseus sheds a tear when he sees poor Argos
(Flash), twenty years old and dying, the first creature
to recognize his master, home at Ithaca after so long.
But Achilles tells the dying Hector that he'll be meat for
the scavenger birds and dogs, and the sacred authors
of the Bible use the dog as a symbol of a base and vicious
person—with the notable exception of the author of the
Book of Tobit. The family dog accompanies Tobias and
the angel Raphael on their long journey, and wags his
tail when they draw near to home again.

That genial love for the dog and his faithfulness
shows up in many fine works of sacred art in the Middle
Ages and the Renaissance. My favorites come from the
hand of the Spanish painter Bartolomé Esteban Murillo.
In his peaceful and yet highly unusual painting of the
Holy Family, Joseph is seated near his workbench while
Mary is seated at her distaff and a basket of wool to
be spun into thread. But Joseph isn't working, and Mary
has turned aside from her work, with a smile. She is
watching Joseph playing with the toddler Jesus, whom
he holds in front of him. Jesus holds a dove in one hand
raised high, and a little white dog, his eyes fixed upon
Jesus, sits and raises his right paw, begging for the dove.
There's the Holy Trinity right there, and the faithful
Christian, asking Jesus to send to him the Holy Spirit.

The same little white dog is found leaping in the air for joy when Murillo's Prodigal Son returns home to his father. Cynics may be dogs, but dogs are not cynics.

Not the sound, which is imitated by our verb, nor the homonym *wring*, which has to do with twisting and turning, but the golden thing you wear on your finger when you're married.

It has a lot of interesting relations, this word, but you wouldn't suspect them at first. We have to find a missing consonant just where a consonant will most slyly sneak off to confuse us: at the beginning.

What was the word for *ring*, back when King Beowulf was giving them out to his faithful thanes? Well, the most common one was *beag*, related to all kinds of words having to do with bowing and bending: a *bagel* is just some bread that Yiddish Germans baked into a ring—or is it boiled? I don't know. Anyway, another word for those bands of honor was *hring*, as when the father in the parable met his wayward son again. Here is the passage in Anglo-Saxon:

> Ða cwæð se fæder to his þeowum, 'Bringað
>   hræðe þone selestan gegierelan and scry-
>   dað hine, ond
> sellað him **hring** on his hand and gescy to his
>   fotum;

Ond bringað an fætt stierc and ofsleað ond
uton etan and gewistfullian;
For þam þes min sunu wæs dead, ond he
geedcwicode; he forwearð ond he is
gemett.'

(Lk 15:22–24)

Allow me to be deliberately archaic in translation:

Then quoth the father to his servants, "Bring
rathe the choicest gear and clothe him,
and give him
rings for his hands and shoes for his feet;
And bring the fatted steer and slay him, and
let us eat and feast our fill;
For this my son was dead, and he is quick
again; he turned astray and he is met
once more."

So there it is, *hring*. The word doesn't start with *r*. It starts with *h*.

So, since Germanic *h* = Italo-Celtic *c (k)*, we are looking for words with *c, r,* and a nasal consonant *(m, n, ng)*. We want words that will remind us of a *hring*. Here are some: Latin *circum, around; corona, crown;* Welsh *crwn, round;* maybe Greek *kyklos, circle,* as in the Circle-Eye, *Kyklops,* the Cyclops. Other English *r* words were really *hr* words, corresponding to Latin *cr*: English *raw* < Old English *hraew;* cf. Latin *cruor: gore, bloodshed.*

When we think of a *ring,* we think of marriage, and rightly so. Feminists used to say that the wedding ring was reminiscent of a manacle; and men who despise

marriage almost as much as the feminists did pick up
the idea when they call a wife the *ball and chain*. But
a ring was a precious gift. Its circularity implied end-
lessness. The gold suggested what was pure and incorruptible and full of light. That you wore it on your hand
suggested an intimate bond. And what is wrong with a
bond? So the poet Spenser, in his *Amoretti,* courts the
young woman who will agree to become his wife, and
knit the knot that ever shall remain. "To enter in these
bonds is to be free," says he.

A rhetorical question from Dame Alice of Bath, translated into modern English by yours truly:

> *And how then can he pay his wife the rent*
> *If he don't use his silly instrument?*

Ol' Alice, five times a widow, is a rich lady, but she's
still hankering after jewels, and that's why she's on the
pilgrimage to Canterbury. She wants a husband, and
she wants some paying up!

Chaucer is having some fun with the Middle English
word *sely,* which was already teetering between two fields
of meaning. The newer meaning, of course, is *silly, sim-
pleminded, foolish.* The older meaning is *blessed:* that is
preserved in Modern German *selig.* The Lord God is *der
Heilige, the Holy One*; but those He blesses are *selig:*

*Selig sind, die da geistlich arm sind; denn das
    Himmelreich ist ihr.*
*Blessed are the poor in spirit, for theirs is the
    kingdom of Heaven.*

(Mt 5:3)

And there is our clue, right there. The stern and serious pagan won't understand it. How can those who are poor in spirit be blessed? To proceed with the Beatitudes, how can you be blessed if everyone is lying about you and persecuting you and handing you over to torment and death? That's silly!

But we are meant to see the blessedness that the world misses. The world takes itself mighty seriously; the world is grave, and the gravity weighs it down. But the saint takes himself lightly. That's what Chesterton said about angels; it's why they can fly. Saint Francis, the poor little man of Assisi, owned nothing but the burlap cloak on his back; and Saint Francis was blessed with the whole world for his home and his chapel. He was, shall we say, *ein seliger Mann, a silly man, a blessed man.* For the foolishness of God is wiser than men.

Serpent

We know that that's a fancy word for *snake,* right?

Not exactly. It's a Latin present participle, turned into a noun. It means "something that creeps," like the creeping things that creep along the ground, created by

the Lord God in the beginning. The Latin *serpens* is
related to Greek *herpeton,* embodying the same idea;
the slithery thing that slithers. I am not sure why the
infection is named *herpes,* but a *herpetologist* is somebody who studies snakes, whether or not the person is
himself a creep.

We might well ask, "Why does the evil one use a serpent for the temptation of Adam and Eve?" Or, if we
read the account as employing an allegorical symbol,
"Why did the inspired author of Genesis use a serpent
to suggest the Tempter?" Serpents naturally give us *the
creeps,* as they slither noiselessly along the ground,
without hands or feet, all mouth and long digestive
tract, with their fangs and their venom. "The serpent
was the subtlest beast of all the field," (see Gn 3:1)
says the author, punning on the Hebrew word for *subtle,* which is almost identical to the Hebrew word for
naked. The serpent then is in two senses all mouth: all
digestion and all concealment, the opposite of what is
open and free. Milton hits upon that idea when Satan
insinuates himself into the serpent, to escape detection
by the angels charged to keep watch over Eden:

> *Of these the vigilance*
> *I dread, and to elude, thus wrapped in mist*
> *Of midnight vapor glide obscure, and pry*
> *In every bush and brake, where hap may find*
> *The serpent sleeping, in whose mazy folds*
> *To hide me, and the dark intent I bring.*

The most common Old English word for the critter,
though, isn't related to what the serpent does, but to
where it does it. The serpent is a *naeddre* in the Old

English Bible of Aelfric, the thing that slinks along below, down there, in the *nether* regions: cf. German *nieder, down.* That's pretty good, for the snake in Genesis: he has come *ab inferis,* from down under, the ultimate Australia. The word survives in Modern English, but in disguise, just like Satan. People said *a naeddre, a naeddre, a naeddre,* for some centuries, until finally the consonant *n* was detached from the word and stuck onto the article: *an adder.* Same thing happened to the *napern,* the thing that Grandma wears around her waist in the kitchen: *an apron.*

Our word today sounds like *think,* and that's appropriate, because the words are related. We move from a verb that means *to seem, to appear,* as in German *duenken,* to the causative verb *to make an image appear to oneself,* in one's own mind, as in *think* (Anglo-Saxon *thyncan,* German *denken*), to a verb meaning *to think good thoughts about someone else,* a causative on top of a causative: Anglo-Saxon *thancian,* German *danken,* Swedish *tak,* English *thank.*

I'm fonder of the Romance language words for giving thanks. *Gratias agimus tibi,* we Catholics sing in the *Gloria* when we return to Latin for the prayers sung on the great feasts; and the word *gratias* suggests the free gift of a loving heart, a gift of praise. A whole host of words in the Romance languages help us to understand the connection between true freedom and love: *grati-tude* is a gift of love in response to a loving gift; *grace* is the free gift of God's favor to man, and even as a description of human beauty and kindness it suggests something free, something in excess of what is strictly necessary. The Latin word is preserved in Italian *gra-zie,* Spanish *gracias,* French *grace.*

It's often said that pride is the worst of sins, but the old poets and theologians suggest that a certain kind of pride is the worst of the worst: the pride that is *thank-less, ungrateful.* That is why Dante reserves the low-est and coldest region of Hell for souls who betrayed their benefactors, Satan being the epitome of those who return evil for good. That sin is everywhere to be found in Shakespeare. So cries King Lear: *"How sharper than a serpent's tooth it is / To have a thankless child!"* So sings the courtier Amiens, who has followed the good Duke Senior into the wilds when the Duke was ban-ished by his ungrateful younger brother:

> *Blow, blow, thou winter wind:*
> *Thou art not so unkind*
> *As man's ingratitude.*

So Milton's Satan, when nobody else is listening, admits that all he had to do in heaven to please the Lord was *"to give him thanks, / The easiest recompense."* It is easy because it is a spontaneous movement of the heart. It is as easy for the grateful heart to pay the "debt" of gratitude as it is for the sun to shine, or for a friend to greet his friend.

When a Frenchman sings thanks to God at Mass, it's *grace a toi;* but when he thanks the waiter at the café, he uses the word *merci,* closely related to our English word *mercy.* That too has an underlying idea of a free gift, but this time the generous reward for service rendered; it's related to our words *merchandise* and *market,* though those words kept to the original Latin track, for words having to do with buying and selling. The idea is that *mercy* is given far in excess of what is really merited. The word in the Latin Bible that is usually translated as *mercy,* however, is completely unrelated: *misericordia,* literally *pity in the heart.* On Thanksgiving, which President Lincoln established as a national feast, we might-should glance away from the football games and the table to think of God's grace and mercy, abounding far beyond our fitful and uncertain attempts to do what is right and just.

Nowadays, the English word *style* suggests that you buy a lot of expensive clothing, or that you pay attention to how the "best" people talk and think and drive and raise their children and decorate their homes and so forth. It comes from Latin *stilus, pen;* and that instrument could be used both for writing and for the more delicate forms of art: think of the hair-thin strokes made by an illuminator of manuscripts.

Writing is taught so badly in our schools, and style not at all, that I hesitate to suggest that my students begin to think of their compositions as, if not works of art, at least works of some linguistic competence that manifest a touch of the artful, here or there. I fear that I'll get prose more desperately mangled than ever, in purple, and even the ultimate horror, the Great Metaphor, lumbering along like a wounded beast and smashing the little reeds of intelligence in his way.

But I will dare. The most immediate way you can develop any kind of style in English is not to break out a thesaurus and take to clogging up your prose with fancy half-synonyms. Ordinary words are fine. The style lies in arranging them.

Word order is the principal means we English speakers use to convey who is doing what to whom. Here are some Latin sentences:

> *Marius gladio Germanum trucidat.*
> *Gladio Germanum Marius trucidat.*
> *Trucidat Marius Germanum gladio.*
> *Germanum trucidat Marius gladio.*

They all mean the same thing: Marius cut down the German by the sword. The word order does not change the function of the words in the sentence. But it *does* change the emphasis, rather along these lines:

> *Marius cut down the German by the sword.*
> *By the sword did Marius cut down the German.*
> *It was Marius who cut down the German by the sword.*
> *It was the German whom Marius cut down by the sword.*

Latin allows for all kinds of playing with word order; English, not so much. And yet, we may still arrange our words in English in an artful way, determining our sentences not only by the bare meaning but by the whole rhetorical effect we wish to convey. Consider this passage from the King James Version:

> *Verily I say unto you, No prophet is accepted in his own country.* But I tell you of a truth, **many widows were in Israel** *in the days of Elias, when the heaven was shut up three years and six months, when great famine was throughout all the land;* But **unto none of them** *was Elias sent, save unto Sarepta, a city of Sidon, unto a woman that was a widow.* And **many lepers were in Israel** *in the time of Eliseus the prophet;* and **none of them was cleansed,** *saving Naaman the Syrian.*
>
> *(Lk 4:24–27)*

Jesus arranged His words with consummate art; it is one of the most telling things in the Gospels. Look at the arrangement of those sentences. The phrases I've put in boldface are parallel with one another, as musical phrases in a well-crafted song echo one another, with variation. Notice that this parallelism requires an unusual reversal of word order in the third verse. Notice also that the long adverbial matter in the second verse is reserved for the end, to cast it in high relief, to stress the misery that Israel suffered at that time; the more usual place for such material would be up front. Let me "revise" so as to write more ordinary sentences, destroying the art and muting the thunder:

> *I say unto you truly, No prophet is accepted in his own country. I tell you truly, that in the days of*

Elias, when the heaven was shut up three years
and six months, and great famine was through-
out all the land, there were many widows in Is-
rael. But Elias was not sent to any of them, save
a widow who lived in Sarepta, a city of Sidon.
And in the time of Eliseus the prophet there were
many lepers in Israel, but only Naaman the Syr-
ian was cleansed.

Let them who have ears to hear, hear.

Almost everyone my age, it seems, has memories of a
very silly horror-soap opera, *Dark Shadows,* in which
one Quentin Collins would occasionally, mutton chops
and all, turn into a werewolf. The idea is pretty ancient.
In Webster's *The Duchess of Malfi,* the evil duke, quite
out of his mind, has bouts of psychotic lycanthropy,
which is just a neato Greek way of saying werewolfism,
or rather *wolfwereism,* because in the Greek word the
wolf comes first. I guess that is what happens when you
kill your brother-in-law and drive your sister mad and
go "batfowling by owl-light." As they used to say in the
old Army training films about certain diseases, "Don't
let *this* happen to you."

Both parts of the *werewolf* are interesting—I mean
the word, not Quentin. I'll look at the *were* today. It is a
generic Anglo-Saxon word for *human being.* If you were

a homicide, that is, if you killed a human being, you might make up for it and prevent a family feud by paying *wergild: man-gold, man-money.* The Latin generic word for human being was *homo* (unrelated to the Greek adjective *homoios,* meaning *same*). That became the base for the Romance language words for grown men: French *homme,* Italian *uomo,* Spanish *hombre.* Here's where things get interesting. Grimm's Law tells us that Latin *h* = Germanic *g,* and in fact we have an Anglo-Saxon word *guma,* meaning *warrior,* that is, *adult male.* Meanwhile, Anglo-Saxon *wer,* human being, is exactly the same word as Latin *vir, adult male* (cf. English *virile;* Irish *fer,* Welsh *gwr*). The words seemed to have crossed: one language took a word for adult male and applied it to human beings generally (Anglo-Saxon), and other languages took a word for human beings generally and applied it to adult males (French, Italian, Spanish).

Feminists may complain, but this sort of thing is natural for human beings. It doesn't imply any superiority in men. Men aren't special; they're generic. Women aren't generic; they're special. Women themselves testify to it even now, when they enter a room full of females and say, "What are you guys up to?" I came upon a delightful instance of this recently when I was traveling in western Newfoundland. I'd been asking a girl at a museum about the accent there and the way they say things.

"So you come into a room," I said, "and you see seven or eight of your friends there, both sexes. And you ask them, 'What are—?" "What are you b'ys doin'!" she laughed. "Boys?" "Yis," she said, in the Newfie way. "B'ys, boys!" "And if they're all girls?" She laughed good and loud. "What are you b'ys doin'!"

The *wolf* part of the word is interesting too. Its Indo-European root gives us Latin *lupus,* source of the word for that flowering plant in the pea family, the *lupin.* A beloved professor of mine who taught me Anglo-Saxon long ago said that the Latin word might have undergone what is called a *taboo deformation.* That is a way to say the word without saying the word. Perhaps you're a hunter in the woods, and the last thing you want to see is a wolf. But you want to use the word, so, lest you say it outright and a wolf show up, you deform it—in this case, reversing the sounds *w* and *l:* so you say *wulp* instead of *lwp.* It's as if you were sleeping in an abandoned house and entertained your friends by telling a story about *goats*—goats that pass through walls and moan and otherwise do the requisite haunting things. So too in English we say *darn* and *shoot* and *jeepers creepers.*

"I am Captain James T. Kirk, of the Starship *Enterprise,*" says the handsome rogue in the yellow shirt, the elevator shoes, and the hidden girdle round the waist. You never saw him in a *kirk,* though, unless it was the chapel of the *Enterprise,* which hardly counts. That's too bad; it might have kept him from peopling the galaxy with Tiberii.

Most people would say that *kirk* is Scots for *church,* and that's true, if we mean Scots English, or the northern dialects generally. Scots English, sometimes called Erse, is utterly different from Scots Gaelic, a Celtic language closely related to Irish, Welsh, Cornish, Breton, and Manx. Plenty of words that in standard English have the sound we spell as *ch* have the sound *k* in Erse. You might see *quhilk* or *quhich* for *which;* and if you tap a certain common tree for its sap and then ferment the oozings, you can drink what the Scots call *birk wine,* and what people in Pennsylvania called *birch beer,* now a soft drink.

The Old English word was *cirice,* and the pronunciation of *c* before the high front vowels *e* and *i* tended to become "palatalized," just as had happened in the change from Latin to Italian: Latin *caelum, heaven,* originally pronounced *kye-lum,* becomes Italian *cielo,* pronounced *chay-lo,* with the sound we spell as *ch.* But in the north of England that palatalization either didn't occur, or it lost out to the older hard *k;* Scandinavian immigration and influence was heavier up there, and they still had their *k*'s in place. So the same word was pronounced in two ways: *cheerich* in the south, *keerk* in the north. We have other *ch / k* doublets in English: *ditch, dike; shirt, skirt;* the oddest is *shriek / screech,* which should be *skriek / shreech,* but people do get confused when they're shreeching or skrieking.

The original word, *cirice,* comes from the Greek *kyriake,* meaning *of the Lord* (cf. the Kyrie, *Lord* have mercy). That word was adopted in the Germanic languages: German *Kirche,* Swedish *kyrka,* English *kirk, church.* But the more common word, from Greek and then Latin, was *ecclesia, a gathering, a calling-together*: Italian *chiesa,* French *eglise,* Spanish *iglesia,* Welsh *eglwys.*

There used to be a verb in English, *to be churched,* referring to the ceremony of purification that a woman underwent some weeks after giving birth. The church was simply the center of social life and of education. When I was a very small boy and my mother took me to Mass during the week, I felt that I was entering a world that held infinite possibilities and infinite mysteries. The church is as Chesterton says: bigger from within than from without.

The ironies of history! The mascot for the University of Virginia is the *cavalier,* bringing to mind images of mustachio'd noblemen in doublets and hose, with big plumed hats and snuffboxes and rapiers. "You mock us!" says Sir Spindleshank, brandishing his rapier. "I shall demand satisfaction!" Wait a while, Sir S. One cavalier at a time. I have to finish playing cards with Sir John Suckling here—the man who invented cribbage.

Yet the word *cavalier* doesn't come from anything so noble. Not ultimately, anyway. It does derive from the French *chevalier, horseman;* and we do have the wonderful English word *chivalry,* which used to describe the mores of a true knight: humility, bravery, gentleness of speech, courtesy, and a readiness to assist women in need, and the poor or the weak. It sounds like the unrelated *shivaree,* what mountain-men do when they serenade a new bride and bridegroom, or play pranks on them. And if you are beset by Apaches on the warpath, you can depend that the *cavalry* is just round the next bend in the river. *Cavalry,* my dear lectors in Catholic churches, is not to be confused with *Calvary,* from Latin *Calvarium,* translating Aramaic *Golgotha, the place of the skull.*

But all these words come from the late Latin word *caballus,* meaning *a dumpy common horse, a hack, a nag.* That came to denote any horse at all: Italian *cavallo,* Spanish *caballo,* French *cheval,* even Welsh *cefyll.* Meanwhile, the old Latin word for horse, *equus* (cf. English *equine*), was lost entirely. That does happen sometimes; the vulgar word replaces the older, more aristocratic word (or the reverse). It happened in English, too. The Anglo-Saxon word for *horse* was *eoh,* a cousin of the Latin word, and possibly also of Greek *hippos* (a *hippopotamus* is a *river-horse; Philip* is a fellow who likes to ride horses). That word is gone, replaced by another word, whose origins we don't really know: *horse* (Norse *hross,* from which C. S. Lewis got his *hrossa* on Mars). And the Germans? They ride *das Pferd.* Don't ask me why.

When English speakers study Latin, they're pleased to recognize the roots of thousands of our words, but sometimes what looks like a cousin or even a brother isn't a kinsman at all, but somebody trying to crash a family reunion. "We're on Uncle Louie's side," declared my scamp of a brother once upon a time, and he and his friend, who were driving home after a round of golf, got a great backyard meal out of it. That's the case with the Latin *dies, diei: day.* It's survived in some common phrases we use straight from the Latin: *carpe diem, per diem;* it's also the source of our word *diurnal,* describing something that happens over the course of one day. The Latin *diurnalis* became the more direct source of the Romance language words for *day:* Italian *giorno,* French *jour;* cf. English *journal,* a daily record. So why shouldn't we expect that *dies* and *day* are related?

Grimm's Law, that's why. Grimm's Law tells us that Latin *d* = Proto-Germanic *t.* But the Old English word for *day* did not begin with *t.* It was *daege;* the initial *d* was later hardened into Modern German *Tag.* The Latin *dies* is, however, related to a host of other words having to do with the brightness of broad daylight, associated with the sky-god. Hence we have Greek *dios,* Latin *divus, divinus* (borrowed for English *divine);* Greek *Zeus* (pronounced *Zdeus*), Latin *Deus, deitas* (English *deity*). None of these is related to *day.*

But they are all related to *Tuesday!* Not to the *day,* but to the *Tues.* For the same Indo-Europeans who worshiped a sky-god moved into northern Europe as they had moved into what became the Greek and Roman world. Again, Latin *d* = Germanic *t.* There it is: the German sky-god, the German *Zeus,* the German counterpart of Roman *Deus-pater* = *Deuspiter* = *Deuppiter* = *Jupiter,* is the god *Tiw,* whose day is the third in the week.

Some people will say that this means that the Christian faith is something merely laid over a solid pagan substrate. They want to say this, because it pleases them. It gives them a reason to ignore the utter uniqueness of the faith and of the person of Christ. But their position is plain silly. If you are a missionary and you wish to evangelize a people, how can you make any headway at all unless you speak their language? And what would be the point of insisting that they change all their names for the days of the week? What would be the point of general confusion and irritation? The Latin Christians did not change the names for most of the days, so we have Italian *martedì, Mars' day, Tuesday;* nor did they bother changing the names of the months, so we have Italian *Agosto,* the month in honor of Caesar *Augustus.* So we in English also have *Wotan's Day = Wotansdaeg > Wednesday, Thor's Day = Thorsdaeg > Thursday,* and *Freia's Day = Freiadaeg > Friday.* Not a big deal.

A Grammatical Interlude:

All sentences require a subject and a verb. True enough. But not all circumstances require that the subject and the verb be expressed.

This is perhaps one time when I'll give elementary school teachers the benefit of the doubt, and let them teach students to write sentences with clearly expressed subjects and verbs. After the lads and lasses have plenty of experience writing real sentences, they can move on to write sentences that look like fragments but really are not, given the context, or they can write fragments indeed, but fragments that get the job done.

Consider the following:

Most dogs whine and carry on when their masters come home from a long trip. **Not Albert.** *He would sit at the end of his lead, wagging his tail, his ears pricked up, but not making a sound, as if to imply, "Well, you're back!* **About time.***"*

The "fragments" here are elliptical sentences. "Not Albert" means "That was not so with Albert." "About time" means "It's about time." These ellipses are swift and emphatic, considerable virtues. Are they only for informal prose? The ancient Romans didn't think so; classical Latin prose is full of elliptical sentences, especially in the squeaky-terse Seneca and Tacitus. The elliptical sentence is especially fine for gnomic declarations of universal strength. Here is a well-known sentence from Augustine:

Amor meus, pondus meum.
My love, my weight.

Concentrated in those four short, ordinary words is a whole theology and anthropology of love. Augustine means, in context, that what he chooses to pursue, the objects of his inclination, are like a weight that tosses him here or there. The desire, if he consents to it, helps to make him what he is, habituating him. We too use metaphors of weight or pull to describe desires both good and evil, as when someone says he is trying to pull himself out of the swamp (which weighs him down), or that the saint bears witness to a joy that is magnetic.

Would Augustine have improved his sentence if he had added the verbs and their modifiers? It would have been clearer out of context. But it would have been quite forgettable. It would not have invited meditation.

Other elliptical sentences that should be dear to the hearts of Catholic Christians: *lex orandi, lex credendi: The law of prayer is the law of belief*; *sursum corda: Lift up your hearts*.

Willy-nilly

English is full of delightful rhyming pairs, usually of two syllables, with the first syllable stressed, often to express a bumptious action, or to cast a humorous light on someone's state of mind. So the *flea-flicker*, in football—and that also is a "rhyming" pair, with the rhyme on the front end—where the quarterback hands it off to the running back, who pitches it to back to the quarterback, who hands it to the cheerleader, who kicks it to the waterboy, who enters the field as a Waterboy Eligible and passes downfield to the umpire who hands it off to the flanker who flips backwards into the endzone, is a *razzle-dazzle* play. But don't call for that play unless you're really *loosey-goosey*, and not at all *wishy-washy.* You'd better keep it *hugger-mugger,* too, or you'll find yourself facing a 3rd and 73.

Willy-nilly is pretty old; in fact, it could only have developed before Modern English standardized our negative. For Jolly Jeff Chaucer, the common negative was *ne,* followed by the verb. If the verb was a form of *be* or *have,* or was one of the modal auxiliaries, the negative and the verb might contract. We still do that: *do not = don't, is not = isn't.* But the negative came first for Chaucer, so, when Alison agrees to commit adultery with handy Nicholas (not *Handy Andy*), she tells him that he'd better be clever, because if her husband ever finds out, *I nam but deed! I'm nothing if not dead!* Here *nam = ne + am.* Other contractions include *noude = ne + coude, could not; nadde = ne + hadde = had not;* and the one that gave us our adverb here: *nill = ne + will, did not want to, did not will.* So someone is dragged off to jail *will he nill he:* whether he will or no. Hence, *willy-nilly.* Latin has its own analogous but independent version of the word and the idea: *nolens volens.*

I hear somebody cry, "But what about *shilly-shally?* And be quick about it! Don't *dilly-dally!*" All right: imagine Fred Flintstone trying to decide whether he's going to tell Wilma that he blew his pay raise on the dinosaur races, or lie about it. The good Fred-angel pops up on one shoulder, saying, "Oh Frederick, surely you would not do so mean and dishonest a thing!" But the bad Fred-angel, with horns and a pitchfork, pops up on the other shoulder, saying, "Don't be a chump, Fred! Who's to know?" So Fred, speaking a very Old English, our genuine Bedrock English, says, *Scyle ic? Sceal ic?* The first is subjunctive, the second indicative;

they mean, roughly, "Should I? Shall I?" So then: the comical verb for not being able to make up your mind: to *shilly-shally.*

An altar at Our Lady of the Assumption in Arichat, Nova Scotia, bears the anagram AM. At first I thought it was MA, abbreviating the name of Mary. But I was wrong; it's AM, short for *auspice Mariae, under the auspices of Mary.*

Auspices aren't hospices; what are they? If Perry Mason is suspicious, you can bet that's not auspicious. What does the word mean?

Our Indo-European ancestors came from the steppes of central Asia. There's not much out there but grassland and sky, so naturally they worshiped sky-gods—generally the most benign in pagan nature-worship, because they don't lend themselves so easily to rites having to do with blood and mud and tombs and dead children. Anyway, when our ancestors migrated down into Greece and Italy they took their sky-gods with them: Zeus, Jupiter. And if sky-gods want to send you a message, what creatures do you think they will send? Not eels or spiders. Birds, of course. That's why the old prophet at the beginning of Homer's *Odyssey* foretells the coming of Odysseus himself: he sees the sign in the flight of birds above, an eagle on the attack.

It's interesting to note, on the side, that nowhere in the Old Testament are the Jews encouraged to do such

things. Soothsayers are severely condemned. That
shows us how desperate Saul has become, and how low
he has fallen, that he should go to the witch of Endor
and ask her to summon up the soul of Samuel. She
obliges him, but when Samuel or a demon imperson-
ating Samuel actually appears, she seems to be even
more surprised than Saul is. Samuel or Pseudo-Samuel
rebukes Saul, who should have spent more time listening to the prophets. But the Greeks and the Romans
looked to the birds. Take the Latin word for bird: *avis*
(cf. English *aviary, aviation*). Now take the Latin verb
for looking: *spectare* (cf. English *inspect, spectacle*).
The ancient Roman soothsayer was a bird-inspector:
avis + *spex* = *auspex*. He takes the bird-inspections:
auspices. Something *auspicious,* then, has good bird-
signs. We would say, changing the metaphors, that it
was *in the cards.*

This is a relatively new word, born in America to describe
social climbers. Now it denotes anybody characterized
by a foolish (though usually ineffectual) refusal to recognize proper authority. A child is uppity when he talks
back to his big brother. If he talks back to his father,
that's worse than being uppity; it's being downright dis-
obedient. A new secretary is uppity when she advises
the long-time secretary on better ways to organize the
files. If she refuses to make the coffee when the older

secretary asks her to, that's worse than being uppity. It's to be disagreeable and insubordinate.

It's pleasant to note that colloquial or slangy words are often the same as sophisticated words, but in different threads. That's the case with *uppity*. When students first encounter Greek tragedy, they're told that the hero is destroyed by a tragic flaw (indistinguishable, for my students from southeastern New England, from a *tragic floor*), which T. F. is denominated *hubris*. What does that mean? Is it a mysterious malady afflicting Greeks in high places? In a way, yes. The word is a nominalization of the adverb *hyper*, meaning *over*, and often suggesting something done too much. If your blood pressure is too high, you have *hypertension;* if you've left the turkey in the oven too long, it's *overdone*. In Old English, someone *uppig* is arrogant; if we'd kept that word, we'd be describing people as *uppy*. Byrhtnoth in *The Battle of Maldon* allows the superior Viking force safe conduct across the causeway, to fight the English on a wide field; the poet says he was moved by his *ofermod:* his *over-mood, high-mindedness*. The brave Englishmen are massacred, but go down nobly and bravely.

Greek words beginning with *h* often correspond with Latin words beginning with *s,* so the Latin counterpart of *hubris* is *superbia, pride,* the worst of the deadly sins. Every schoolboy used to know the name of the last Etruscan king of Rome, driven out by the people after years of his overbearing rule, the rebellion finally set aflame when his son raped Lucretia, the wife of a Roman senator. Lucretia swore her husband and his friends to avenge her death. Then she slew herself, lest her example give less virtuous Roman women an excuse for adultery. The name of that king: Tarquinius *Superbus,* Tarquin the Proud.

But really, *hubris, superbia,* and *ofermod* all mean *uppity,* in structure and form. It's nice to take those fancy words down a peg or two!

It's an odd word, this. We have it in Old English, pretty much as it is now. In the epic *Christ,* God creates the world and gives joys to all His angelic retainers and to Adam: *dreamas bedelde,* says the poet: *he dealt out joys.* But in *Beowulf,* when the monster Grendel, alone on the moor, hears the music of the harp and the singing and the joyous laughter coming from the great hall of Heorot, he hates it all, because he is *dreamas bidaeled, deprived of joys.*

The word for *dream,* in Old English, was *swefn* (rhyming with *seven*). So the speaker in the momentous poem *The Dream of the Rood* tells us that he has experienced *swefna cyst, the choicest of dreams.* That word survived well into Middle English, too. The author of *Pearl,* writing in the late fourteenth century, uses it to describe what happens when he falls asleep at the grave of his little daughter. *My body on balke ther bod in sweven,* he says, *my body abode on the mound in a dream.* If we remember that English and Greek are on opposite sides of the *s / h* divide, and if we remember Grimm's Law associating Greek *p* with Germanic *f,* we see that *swefn* is a sibling of *hypnos* (cf. English *hyp-notize;* Welsh *huno, sleep*). Latin speakers assimilated that labial *p* to the following nasal *n,* giving us the *mn* in *somnium, dream* (cf. French *songe,* Italian *sogno,* pronounced *sohn-yo*).

Anyhow, at some time in the Middle Ages, the word *dream* replaced the older word *sweven,* and nobody really knows when or how. My guess is that the dream-vision poems, so common and so deeply religious, sug-gested a connection between dreaming and joy. If that is so, then the *dream* as we know it is first a *holy vision,* as the prophet says when the Lord promises that the young shall see visions and the old men shall *dream dreams.*

There is one old man whom we often find asleep in paintings of the Nativity. It's Saint Joseph, of course. I think that there's a gentle jocularity in that. Joseph is older than Mary, he's had a long and weary journey, the excitement has proved too much for him, and he has fallen asleep. Chaucer plays upon that convention in *The Miller's Tale,* when the daft old carpenter John has been persuaded that Noah's or Noel's Flood is coming once again. He knocks out a hole in the gable of the second story, hangs three big kneading troughs from the rafters, one for himself, one for his frisky young wife Alison, and one for the devious undergraduate Nicho-las, where they are supposed to go to sleep, waiting for the waters to rise. When John the carpenter falls asleep and snores away—because his head is in an awkward position—Alison and Nicholas scramble downstairs to play.

But in the paintings, as Chaucer certainly knew, Saint Joseph is asleep not just because he is old and tired. He is asleep because he is dreaming dreams. All of the instructions he receives in the Gospels come to him in dreams, nor does he speak a single word. It is impossible to imagine a state in which one could be less forward with himself and more receptive to the Word of God, than that in which Joseph dreamed the dreams through which God spoke to him.

The victors write the history, as the saying goes. So too the people in the city get to praise city life and city manners and make fun of the people in the country. There are exceptions: Horace's country mouse has the better of the city mouse. But generally, "city" words bring praise, and "country" words are subject to anything from gentle fun to downright contempt.

Our word today, *urbane,* is just such a city-word. It refers, literally, to somebody who is *urban,* who is at home in the city. It even provided the Romance languages with a sophisticated name: Latin *Urbanus,* Italian *Urbano,* French *Urbain.* I see the urbane man in my mind's eye, sitting at his usual table at Twenty One, sipping *pinot noir* and discoursing on the merits of the latest prima donna to sing the title role in *La Traviata.*

The opposite of *urbanus* is *rusticus,* English *rustic,* from the *rus* or the outback (cf. English *rural*). Now we might admire the rustic charm of a log cabin in Vermont—so long as the coffee shop is nearby and

the neighbors don't keep swine. But for most of its history in English, *rustic* was roughly equivalent to *back-
woods:* a rustic was a hick, a hillbilly, a redneck (notice,
by the way, the sniffy urban contempt for manual labor,
evident in that last term: a man gets a red neck from
working outdoors in the sun). We call someone who has
spent his life in study *erudite,* and that literally means
that he's had the *coarse* rubbed out of him by education. He used to be a *raw* fellow, *rough* enough, but he
ain't no more. But if that smarty-pants has bad manners
anyway, we won't call him *urbane.* We call him *crude,*
like something that comes straight from the ground,
uncooked, like a muddy head of cabbage.

For all that, we have an even worse example of city
snobbery in our word *villain,* which originally meant
somebody who worked on the farm, on the manor, the
villa. Chaucer's Knight *never yet ne spake ne vilenye*
to anybody, a neat triple negative there; he was a par-
agon of *cortesie* (note: a virtue you practice at *court*).
He was soft-spoken and meek. By Shakespeare's time,
the hunchback murderer Richard III could say, "I am a
villain," and nobody would think he meant that he dug
potatoes or swore a lot.

"He *exudes confidence,*" we see in the papers; in fact,
confidence is about the only thing that anybody ever
exudes. The trouble is that that's a singularly odd

phrase, almost comical. For the word literally means to *sweat*. Maybe he sweats confidence. What a pheromonal phenomenon! I have heard, though, that the sweat of a man can calm the nerves of a roomful of women. If that is true, ladies, I offer my services at a most reasonable rate. Or I suggest a new business for enterprising young men. The Scungilli Brothers will agree to sit in your office in the summer, unwashed, with their feet up on the desk and their arms locked behind their heads, eating hot peppers and washing them down with beer, at only fifty dollars an hour!

The key thing to remember—not about Marco and Sonny Scungilli, but about our word—is that spelling sometimes hides a sound that is really still there. That's the case with the *ex* in *exude*. It absorbs the *s* of the following word. So *exudo* = *ex* + *sudo, I sweat out.* So *expecto* = *ex* + *specto, I gaze forth,* and *existo* = *ex* + *sisto, I stand forth.* Most of the time, though, there wasn't a consonant to absorb, so that *extraho* = *ex* + *traho, I draw out.*

Latin *sudor, sweat,* seems to be related to a passel of words having to do with moisture. Again we remember the *s / h* divide between Latin and Greek, so we can see that *sudor* is kin to Greek *hydor, water.* Celtic lies on the Greek side of that divide, so Welsh, losing the light initial syllable, has *dwr, water.* So then, what can we exude? The sour smell of arrogance? Fear, which a dog can sniff out? Something unpleasant, anyway.

There are two instances of sweat in Scripture that seem to comprehend the whole history of salvation. When the Lord judges Adam in Eden, He says, "In the sweat of your brow you shall eat bread." I find that part of what's called Adam's Curse to be fascinating, because the curse conceals a great promise. Adam will have to work hard, no doubt, and sweat while he hacks away at dry soil with his spade, or tries to carve it up with a stick-plow hitched to the shoulders of an ox. But from that sweat will come *lehem, bread:* the first use of the word in Scripture, looking forward to the manna from heaven, and the bread of life, *lehem-chaim,* which Jesus not only promises but which He Himself is. And how do you make bread from those hard nutty grains on the ear of wheat or barley? You thrash them and winnow them to free them from the stalks and the chaff, and then you crush them under a millstone, to grind them to powder. And so it was that Jesus became the bread of life to us, as he prayed in the Garden of Gethsemane, preparing for the ultimate sacrifice, and as the beloved physician Luke says, His sweat became like drops of blood on the ground.

pterodactyl

"Daddy, what's that animal floating up there in the sky?" "That, Thag, is the feather-finger." Little Thag Simmons knits his brows. "That's a funny name. Why do we call it that?" "Well, it's because his feathers aren't really feathers and his fingers aren't really fingers. You see, he's a lizard on his way towards becoming a bird. At least that's what they say. Son, these are exciting times we are living in!"

It's good to turn bigshot scientific names into down-to-earth English names, just to see the fun that naturalists are having when we're not looking. The *pterodactyl* is a case in point. It's made up of two Greek words, *pteros* for *feather* and *dactylos* for *finger*. Now, the Greeks pronounced what we'd consider impossible consonant combinations. They didn't say *terodactyl*. They said *pterodactyl, ppppterodactyl,* or would have said it had there been any. If we keep that in mind, and apply Grimm's Law, which reminds us that Greek *p* = Germanic *f* and Greek *t* = Germanic *th,* we'll see straightaway that *pteros* is just our word *feather.*

What about the *dactyl, finger?* It's also a term for a certain poetic meter. The Romans and Greeks wrote their epics in *dactylic hexameter:* so what's a dactyl? That's easy. It's a finger-rhythm. Look at your finger, those of you who do not play with fireworks. It's divided into three, isn't it? One long joint, followed by two short joints, each about half the size of the long joint. So a dactyl is long-short-short, as in *PRAISE to the LORD, the alMIGHty, the KING of creAtion.* The Romans and Greeks figured, too, that two shorts were equal to one long, so they allowed a "dactyl" to be LONG-LONG also, adding a great deal of variety to their poetic lines.

Speaking of fingers: the flower we call the foxglove is, in German, *Fingerhut, finger-hat,* a delightfully picturesque way to describe the small clustering flowers on the plant's long stalk. Scientists discovered that a drug made from the foxglove had profound effects on the heart. Their Latin name for the drug recalls the German finger-hat: *digitalis.*

"What God hath joined together . . ."
"Greater love than this hath no . . ."
"What shall it profit a . . ."
"Somebody doth not live by bread alone . . ."
"Let us make, er, in our own image . . ."
*"Quick, send for help! We need a word, we need
    a word!"*
"This is a job for—Inclusive Man!*"*

No other word will do. We need a word that is not just
general but universal. Out goes *human being,* which
is singular but not a universal term. Out goes *person,*
same reason. We need a word that is concrete, not
abstract. Out goes *humanity.* We need a word that is
singular, embracing all human beings in one, at once.
Out go *men and women, human beings, people, we,
all, humankind,* and even *mankind.* We need a word
that is intensely personal. We need to see all human
beings as represented in one, not a collective, not a
quality, not a generality, but a singular, concrete, personal, all-embracing representative. In English only
man remains. There is no other word, nor any combination of words, that can perform that linguistic work.

To disallow the universal and genuinely inclusive
use of *man* is to forbid the very *thought* that all human
beings may be represented in one. That is not only

arbitrary; it is not only, for a Christian, theologically incoherent; it is an affront to the mind of man. It is an anthropological absurdity. When *man* is used to denote all and each, what is implied is that there is nothing *special* about the adult male. He is the generic thing. All others are special in relation to the generic term. *Child* is marked for age, *woman* is marked for sex, *human being* is marked for a quality shared by all of us, but it too *specifies*, as does the phrase *divine being*. I should have a hard time calling Hitler a *human* being, but no problem indicating him as *man:* proud, foolish, cruel, God-denying, pathetic *man.*

But is it just? Of course it is. The most obvious justification is necessity; as I've shown, no other word will do. Attempts to avoid it make hash out of statements of breathtaking conciseness and power:

> *Not by bread alone doth man live, but by every word that cometh from the mouth of God.*
>
> *(see Dt 8:3)*

It is absolutely essential, in that sentence, to balance the singular, universal, personal term *man*—meaning each one of us, and all of us together, as one—against God. Let us look at the bad alternatives:

> *We do not live by bread alone, but by every word that comes from the mouth of God.*

Who are *we?* Christians alone? Christians and Jews? Everybody, in a group? It's not clear. The balance is lost, too—the sense that *man* is nothing without *God.* Let's try another:

*Human beings do not live by bread alone, but by
every word that comes from the mouth of God.*

That is a general statement. But its universality is
doubtful. We may say all kinds of things about *human
beings* which are generally but not universally true. We
have also lost the intense focus on the personal, which
here is blurred in the great big plural corral. Not good.
What about this:

*A person does not live by bread alone, but by
every word that comes from the mouth of God.*

Well, now we have a singular balanced against a singular, but it still isn't universal. It's indefinite. Which
person? Any person? Are we also talking about angelic
persons? We have lost the light cast upon the ontological
difference between *man* here and *God* there, because
the reason why *man* does not live by bread alone is not
that he is a *person*—God too is personal—but that he
is *man.*

Humanity? The same failing that *human beings* suffers from, and abstract to boot. The pronoun *one?* The
same failing that *a person* suffers from, and worse.

For the record, I don't care, either, for circumlocutions cobbled together to avoid implying the obvious.
I call them *policemen* because that's what they are. I
note, by the way, that women themselves, playing basketball, use *man-to-man* defense, and women in NASA
speak about *manned* spacecraft, and women archaeol-
ogists distinguish the natural from the *man-made,* and
so forth. Here is a rule less grammatical than tautologi-
cal. Never seek to placate the implacable.

A Grammatical Interlude:

The first time I heard of expletives was in the good Sister Carmine's sixth grade class. No, she was not referring to obscenities or profanities. I encountered the word in that sense when I read about the Watergate investigations, which uncovered many a text quoted in newspapers with the occasional interruption: (expletive deleted). Those texts, with the expletives deleted, made our rulers look like a gang of delinquents rumbling in an alley over who stole the keg of moonshine, and who made what crack over whose girl's purple tattoo.

But Sister Carmine of happy memory defined the expletive as a placeholder subject, an empty word to occupy the position, while the true subject came later. Our language has two common expletives: *there, it.* Latin didn't have them. Consider the following sentences:

> *Cantare Domino bonum est. Singing to the Lord is good.*

> *Bonum est cantare Domino. It is good to sing to the Lord.*

We see that the two sentences say much the same thing, but with a different emphasis. The first concentrates on evaluating the action of singing to the Lord: singing to the Lord is good, not bad. The second declares the goodness up front, and opens out toward focusing on the Lord's glory and holiness. The expletive flashes to the hearer or reader that a long subject may be coming, which it would be inconvenient to cast in front of the verb:

> *It is a dreadful thing for the slaveholder to consider that God is just.*

In fact, if we were to revise this sentence so as to remove the expletive and the verb *to be,* we'd make hash of it, robbing it of its power and shifting the emphasis away from the justice of God to the feelings of the slaveholder:

> *Slaveholders must dread to consider that God is just.*

There are times, we see, when fewer words are not better words. If you find yourself beginning many of your sentences with placeholders, you should ask what your true subjects and verbs are, and revise accordingly. But it would be silly to replace them all, by formula.

By the way, if you want to impersonate Boris Badunov on the old Bullwinkle show, just omit your expletives, make your voice go *basso profondo,* and think evil: *Ees good to keel moose and squirl.* Is good to know grammar. Is delight, to play with style. Is, no?

Verse

When a Welsh schoolmaster asks to see his pupil's work, he asks for his *gwersi.* That seems to be a loan word directly from Latin *versus,* from way back in the days before King Arthur, when the Romans conquered southern Britain and brought reading and writing with them. What were a schoolboy's lessons? *Verses*—in poetry. Nowadays poems are frilly things for people to express what they are pleased to call their thoughts, but in those days, the poetry of Virgil was central to a Roman lad's education in history, rhetoric, personal virtue, and patriotism. Poetry remained central to western education until quite recently. Ordinary men and women, farmers, carpenters, housewives, would treasure in their memories hundreds of verses of poetry and hymns, not to mention verses from Scripture—note the assumption that Scripture too was poetic, as indeed it is. Now all of that is gone, and instead of Watts' *When I Survey the Wondrous Cross,* or Bunyan's *Who Would True Valor See,* not to mention Scripture itself, or Milton, or Pope, we have

> *Rice-a-Roni, it's flavor can't be beat!*
> *Rice-a-Roni, the San Francisco treat!*

But for all that, we still say that an expert is well-*versed* in his field, as if he had acquired his knowledge of the periodic table by poetry.

The idea behind the Latin *versus* is interesting too. A verse is a verse, and not a curse, because it *turns,* in predictable ways. Unlike modern poets, the old masters didn't flip a coin to determine when their lines should end, but followed rules that determined when the turns from one line to the next would come—literally, rules of *versification.* The Latin word is related to a huge family of words having to do with turning. That becomes clearer to us if we pronounce the word in its original way: *wair-sus.* The *wer-* suggests the turn. In English, to turn back is to go *back-ward;* in Latin, then in English, to *pervert* is to turn something inside out. In Old English, *wyrd* means *fate, destiny, the way things turn out:* and that's why the witch-sisters in Macbeth are really *weird.* It's not that they hang out on the blasted heath and toss eyes of newts and toes of frogs and livers of blaspheming Jews into cauldrons, while singing through bad teeth. It's that they know how things are going to *turn.*

One of the great things about learning Latin is that you finally learn English. Our language is most unusual, in that five hundred years ago we began importing a tremendous number of words straight into English from Latin. Just in that last sentence we have the Latin words *import* and *tremendous,* the latter meaning "causing tremors of awe or fear." It's fun to use the Latin to peer into a word's inner sanctum, where it guards its semantic history.

So then: *recalcitrant.* The heart of the word is the Latin *calx, heel.* I believe that the word is cognate with Anglo-Saxon *hela, heel* (Grimm tells us that Latin *c* = Germanic *h*). Latin speakers evidently sang a song, "The heelbone's connected to the—limestone," the secondary meaning of *calx,* whence we derive *calcium* and, from the Saxons borrowing from their Latin teachers or masters, *chalk.* But the prefix *re-* suggests either a repetition or, as here, a backward motion: cf. *recoil,* when the fire of the gun jolts you backwards, or *rebuff,* when you brush somebody back, or *renege,* when you go back on a promise. A mule is characteristically *recalcitrant:* as we say in English, he hangs back, he *digs in his heels.*

When we know these meanings, we can suggest a concrete and robustly descriptive sense underlying what might usually be felt as an abstract word. Milton, Pope, Hopkins, and T. S. Eliot do this all the time. *Instruct me,* cries Milton to the Holy Spirit as he begins his mighty poem, the Spirit who prefers *before all temples th' upright heart and pure.* What does he mean? If we don't know our Latin, we suppose that he's praying that the Spirit will teach him, will give him instruction in divine and ancient things. That's true enough. But if we do know our Latin, we see that Milton has engaged in a bilingual pun of some theological profundity. The Latin verb *instruere* literally means *to build up* (cf. English *construction*). So Milton is asking that the Spirit will build him up into a worthy temple; the prayer is for both knowledge and holiness.

In one of the quietest and most profound of his lyric poems, *Childhood,* George Herbert prays for a simplicity that will be proof against all of the temptations with which we are beset by physical and spiritual age. "Let me be soft and supple to thy will," he says. That word *supple* suggests the tender flesh of a child, soft, easily yielding. It is the same idea in Gerard Manley Hopkins' poem *The Bugler's First Communion.* The lad who comes to Father Hopkins for instruction in the Catholic faith yields to his teaching gently, "as a pushed peach." But *supple* suggests more than softness. Its Latin ancestor, as Herbert knew and expected his reader to know, is *supplex:* literally, *folded from below.* It's what you do when you make yourself small, child-size, by falling upon bended knees. In that posture you are most truly a *suppliant,* and your prayers are *supplications.* Aged knees are sometimes not very supple. That may be a problem of the accretion of calcium in the joints. Aged souls are sometimes not very supple, either. That is a problem of the encrustations of sin. Bend, stubborn knees!

Stupid

It's hard not to like our only word that rhymes with *Cupid,* and actually *ought to do so,* so foolish are we when the bold boy shoots us with the arrows.

The brilliant and urbane and wicked Emperor Frederick II, ruling from his palaces in Sicily and Cosenza, was called, or had himself called *Stupor Mundi.* He didn't mean, *Stupidity of the World.* He meant that his glory would strike the beholder dumb with wonder. It would, literally, *stupefy* the beholder. The *stupor* then, is active and passive in sense at once, referring to the world's reaction and to Frederick's causing it. Dante admired Frederick and put him in Hell with the materialist heretics. He admired a second cousin of Frederick a lot more—the man who really ought to have been called the Wonder of the World, then and still now: Saint Thomas Aquinas.

Over the course of the centuries, the word *stupor* lost its sense of marvel, and, retaining its sense of speechlessness, slud over to kinda mean being reely dum. That sense, though, always was lurking in the wings, waiting to take over. The Latin suffix -*idus* almost always refers to something at least faintly unpleasant or feeble or ugly. The pejorative nuances survive in English: *putrid, pallid, horrid, flaccid, lurid, viscid, acid, acrid, stolid, rabid, torrid, humid, tumid, vapid, timid, rancid, fetid, torpid.* Some are neutral: *solid.* A few are words of praise: *lucid, valid.*

When I was young, our English textbooks advised us to pronounce the vowel in *stupid* as a diphthong, just as in *Cupid: styoopid.* But in northeastern Pennsylvania, that diphthong in such words has all but disappeared if it follows any consonant other than *c, f, m, p.* So we said *stoopid;* and the university in North Carolina is *Dook,* and the lies paraded on television are called the *noos,* and you listen to *toons* at the dance hall. It may have been stoopid, but so it was.

Another word for the transcendent sense of wonder is the Latin verb *mirare,* which gives us the fine neuter plural noun *mirabilia,* often to be found in the Old Testament to describe the wondrous things God has done. I like the verb best in Shakespeare's coined name, which, like so much else that Shakespeare thought and wrote, has entered our language and culture forever: *Miranda,* a Latin gerundive meaning *She who is to be admired, she who arouses wonder.* And she does, too: she is beautiful and pure and holy and filled with readiness to love. Hers are among the most poignant words in all of the master's plays. She suddenly sees for the first time in her life a room full of human beings. She does not know who they are; two of them are wicked villains, one is the repentant father of the young man she has met and to whom she has pledged her love, and one is a good old counselor and friend of her banished father, Prospero. But all she sees is our grandeur:

> *O wonder!*
> *How many goodly creatures are there here!*
> *How beauteous mankind is! O brave new world*
> *That hath such creatures in it!*

"'Tis new to thee," says her father, sadly and gently.

Marlon Brando, in a Brooklyn accent, standing upon the marble steps of the Senate house in Rome:

> *But Brutus sez that Caesar was ambishus,*
> *An' Brutus is an honorable man,*
> *So are they all, all honorable men.*

What's wrong with being ambitious? Does Marc Antony merely mean, "Brutus says that Caesar was aspiring to a higher office than the one he already had," higher than dictator for life?

No, not merely that. That would have been bad enough. But *ambition* was considered to be a vice in itself, just as arrogance and avarice still are, here and there. It reveals something about our own lean and hungry ethos of "achievement" that we Americans have turned an insult into praise. Shakespeare viewed ambitious men as dangerous and unreliable. So did the ancient Romans. So did Milton. Here is what Satan says when he sees the sun for the first time, and when his fellow devils aren't around to hear him admit that his rebellion was foolish and ungrateful:

> *O thou that with surpassing glory crowned*
> *Lookst from thy sole dominions like the god*
> *Of this new world, at whose sight all the stars*
> *Hide their diminished heads, to thee I call,*
> *But with no friendly voice, and add thy name*
> *O Sun, to tell thee how I hate thy beams*
> *That bring to my remembrance from what height*
> *I fell, how glorious far above thy sphere,*
> *Till pride and worse ambition threw me down,*
> *Warring in heaven against heaven's matchless*
>   *King.*

So did Swift, so did Pope, so did Johnson, so did Dickens and Tennyson and Browning. We are the odd ones out.

The inner meaning of the Latin word, if anything, makes us look all the worse. Latin *ambitiosus* is composed of three elements. The first, *amb-*, suggests a motion round and round, helter skelter, hither and yon; so someone who is *ambidextrous* can throw with both the right and the left hand. The third, the suffix *-osus*, suggests being filled with something, usually to one's harm or shame. So the *miles gloriosus* of Roman comedy is the swaggering soldier all full of his glory. To be *curiosus* is to be full of *cura* or painstaking trouble, about something that is not worth it or is not your business. Something *speciosus* is full of a shining superficiality: English *specious*. A *bilious* man is full of bile; a *supercilious* man is always glaring down at you from his *cilia*, his eyelashes. So what's the *ambitious* man full of?

He's full of *it*: the middle element of the word. This is just the verb *ire, to go*; *exit = he goes out*; *ambit = he goes around* (cf. English *itinerant, journeying,* often on foot). Literally, then, he's a man who goes round and round all the time. Doing what? Why does he—notice that we have the same idea—*make the rounds*? To canvass for votes, that's why. Yes, instead of merely stating his convictions and letting the electors decide, he visits here and visits there, glad-handing with the farmers and jesting with the suburbanites, promising bread and circuses to the urban underclass—acting as a perfect *politician*, one who relies not on truth or fidelity to promises but on *policy*, what we would call *political strategy*.

So, in Shakespeare's time, to call Caesar an *ambitious politician* was nigh unto calling him Satan in the flesh. And what is Milton's Satan, if not an ambitious politician?

andrew

The name of this most amiable of the apostles was Greek, *Andreas.* When Jesus asked the apostles whether they had any food with them for the crowds, Saint Andrew came forward and said, "Here is a lad with two barley loaves and five fishes." My friend, the Orthodox priest Patrick Henry Reardon, has written that we can imagine Andrew noticing the boy and having had a pleasant chat with him, and that's why he was ready to reply. It's the same sociable Andrew who said to his brother, "Hey Simon, come on over here! We've met the Messiah!" So maybe Andrew should be the patron saint of easy conversations.

But why did Andrew, a Jew, have a Greek name? Well, that was common enough; many Jews had both Hebrew and Greek names, since Greek was the common language of trade and government in the east. People who live near port cities or trade routes are usually masters of a couple of languages. The apostle *Nathaniel,* whose name means *gift of the Lord* in Hebrew, was also called *Bartholomew,* which was a combination of Hebrew *bar* (*son of;* Peter is *Simon bar-Jonah*) and Greek *Ptolomaeus,* meaning *warlike;* in English we know the name as *Ptolemy,* as of the great ancient mathematician who mapped the stars and measured their motions. *Andreas* means *manly:* it's the Andrew-hormones, so to speak, that give us men hairy chests and deep voices and easy-to-build muscles.

What interests me about this name is that we may have a spelling-pronunciation: that is, a pronunciation that derives from how people came to *see the word spelled,* rather than how it had always been pronounced. The semivowels *w, y* were quite unstable in the dialects of early modern English, and invited a strange variety of spellings. For instance, in the official proceedings concerning the death of the playwright and double agent Christopher Marlowe (stabbed through the eye in a barroom), the young man is sometimes named *Morley;* another variant is *Marley.* That's in the late sixteenth century; the seventeenth century poet Thomas *Carew* pronounced his name *Cary.* Nor do we see the *oo* vowel in the name Andrew in any of the nearby European languages: German *Andreas,* Norse *Anders,* Italian *Andrea* (pronounced *ahn-DRAY-a;* to this day it is solely a man's name in Italy), Spanish *Andres,* French *Andre.*

So then, was the name *Andrew* pronounced, in early modern English, *Andry?* Quite possibly. There's evidence in the Anglicized surname *Landry,* which is just French *L'Andre.* There's also the diminutive *Andy.* And then there's Andrew's fellow apostle, Bartholomew. *That* is almost certainly a case of spelling-pronunciation. We're pretty sure that Marlowe or Morley, in his play *The Massacre at Paris,* pronounced it *Bartlemy:* so it was the *Saint Bartlemy's Day Massacre.* From that pronunciation we get the surname *Bartleby,* as in Melville's melancholy scrivener.

Perhaps I should now give cases of names ending in *-ew* that were pronounced as we'd expect, but I should prefer not to. (ed. note: If you don't get the joke, read Melville's story.)

The word *joy* wasn't around in Old English times. In fact, the letter *j* wasn't around, nor was the sound it made. There were words for the idea: *dream* (yes, what we now use to denote things that go bump in our heads in the night), *blysse* (our *bliss,* now limited to considerations of heaven, or connubial happiness), and others.

C. S. Lewis, recounting the apprehension of something inexpressibly good and beautiful that came to him in his youth when he read of the death of the good Norse god Balder, called it *Surprised by Joy.* It was his memory of that fleeting taste of joy that helped to bring him to the Christian faith. Indeed, when I consider my secular colleagues, their lives seem sometimes pleasant, sometimes arid, sometimes orderly, sometimes chaotic, but always untouched by joy. Nobody is surprised by *pleasure;* the only surprising thing about pleasure is that it is often not very pleasing. People pursue *happiness,* though usually in the wrong places. When they attain some measure of it, they feel some satisfaction, but no surprise. But joy, by its nature, cannot be planned, cannot even be pursued. It is a grace. It is brought by the Spirit of God, who bloweth where He listeth.

The beautiful English word itself—so perfectly expressive of the feeling and yet, in its brevity, suggesting more than it expresses—derives from the Latin *gaudere, to rejoice.* Most of the Latin words beginning with *ga, go, gu* retained the hard *g* sound in Italian and French, but *g* before the diphthong *au* seems to have gone the route of *g* before the front vowels *e* and *i:* so Latin *gentis* becomes Italian *gente, people,* and French *gent,* pronounced *zhaw(n),* or, in the Middle Ages, *zhawnt.* Latin *gaudium, joy,* became the lovely Italian *gioia (JOY-ah),* and French *joie,* which during the centuries when the Norman French were ruling England would have been pronounced rather like *zhoy:* hence English *joy.* The word is all over the old English Christmas carols, as is right and just.

An old poet I once knew used to say that *cleave* was the only word that was the antonym to its own homonym. That is, *cleave* number one is the opposite of *cleave* number two. A couple of examples. In Tennyson's *Idylls of the King,* Mark of Cornwall catches his nephew Tristan unawares. Tristan has returned to Cornwall—bad decision—after having left Mark's wife Iseult, with whom he had carried on an adulterous affair, for Brittany, where he wedded another Iseult, she of the white hands. He has now left the second Iseult for the first Iseult, but Mark sneaks up behind him with an ax:

> *"Mark's way," said Mark, and clove him through the brain.*

That would mean that Tristan's one head has become two—not a good day for Tristan. But when the Pharisees asked Jesus about another kind of splitting, divorce, Jesus replies that it is not part of God's original plan. He quotes Genesis: "And for this reason a man shall leave his mother and his father and *cleave* unto his wife, and they two shall be one flesh" (see Gn 2:24).

So *cleave* number one means that something is split in two, and *cleave* number two means that two things become one; they stick together.

Were people confused? No; it's just that two entirely different verbs merged, because they were similar in sound. The first, *cleofan,* was a "strong" verb, forming its past tenses by vowel change: *cleofan, claf, clufon, clofen.* That verb gives us the past forms *clave* and *clove,* the latter still to be met with now and again, and the past participle *cloven.* But now the more typical past is the dental *cleft,* by analogy with *leave* and *bereave* (and *heave;* the word *heft* has lost its past verbal sense and is now solely a noun). We talk about a *cleft chin* and a *cleft palate,* but instead a *cloven oak.* The second verb, *clifian,* was a humdrum weak verb, related to other *cl-* words having to do with clinging: *cling, clay, clot.*

Those sticky words are cousins of several Latin and Greek words beginning with *gl:* sticky *gluten* (cf. English *glue*).

This is a word with a fascinating history. It has almost become its own opposite. In the Middle English poem *Pearl*, the dreamer describes a beautiful landscape stippled with blossoms blue and red and *blayke*—black flowers? bleak flowers? No; *white* flowers! The Old English *blac* originally did not mean *black*, but *white!* The idea that seems to link black and white is that they are both without color. Anyway, what if you want to make something white? You add the causative infinitive suffix to your adjective, and after a couple of sound changes, you have *blaecan, to bleach*. Eventually, *white* took over, as also in German (*weiss*), and the word *black* assumed most of the work of the older *sweart* (English *swart, swarthy*, meaning *well-tanned*, and hence, by association, muscular, as of a man who does hard work outdoors in the sun; cf. also German *schwarz*). *Bleak* came to describe something pale, then gray, then dim, then almost dark.

Is it related to words in Latin and Greek? Plenty. Walk it back through Grimm: Germanic *b* = Latin *f*, Greek *ph*; Germanic *k* = Latin, Greek *g*. So we have the fiery river of the underworld, the Greek *Phlegethon*, and the flame-flower *phlox*, and Latin *fulgere, to flash* (cf. English *refulgent*), and *flagrare, to burn*, as in a rip-roaring bonfire: so the general and his tart were discovered *in flagrante delicto*, literally *in the crime while it was still a-burning*.

Now, we know that a lot of French words entered English during the centuries after the Norman Conquest. But the word-trade went in the other direction, too. From the Germanic words for white and whitening, we get Italian *bianco,* Spanish *blanco,* French *blanc.* But then those words, in furrener-dugs, stowed away on some boat and came back to English: *blanch,* to boil a vegetable till it loses its color, or to turn white with shame or fear. There's also *blank,* which now means that you haven't used your number two lead pencil to mark the circle on your daily standardized test in school: you have left it without color, empty: *blank.* Unrhymed iambic pentameter, the most common meter used by the great English poets, and therefore unknown to students in American schools, is called *blank verse;* it has the music of the meter, but not the color of rhyme.

This is a word whose secondary meanings have faded a little, but they are still quite alive, and you have to be aware of them if you're going to understand its use in poetry.

Something that is *dear* is, literally, *precious, costly.* Your *dearling,* that is to say your *darling,* is the one you prize, the one you deem precious. So Milton has Beelzebub suggesting to his fellow politicians that, instead of attacking the Most High, they conspire to tempt a couple of naked people:

This would surpass
Common revenge, and interrupt his joy
In our confusion, and our joy upraise
In his disturbance, when his darling sons,
Hurled headlong to partake with us, shall curse
Their frail Original, and faded bliss,
Faded so soon.

If we remember the notion of *price* hiding beneath the noun *darling,* which Beelzebub uses so scornfully, we may also remember the Savior who will come to pay the price of our sin.

So Spenser, in his sonnet commemorating Easter:

This joyous day, dear Lord, with joy begin,
And grant that we for whom thou diddest die,
Being with thy dear blood clean washed from
*   sin,*
May live forever in felicity.

That second *dear* at once delivers the image of the *precious* blood of Christ, and of the *dear* cost He paid, and the *dear* love we bear for Him in return.

Some old-timers still will use *dear* in a wholly monetary sense: "That steak is too dear!" We preserve the notion, too, in such constructions as "You'll pay dearly for this!" The German relative, *teuer,* means *costly,* with a secondary association of personal esteem; otherwise, the word for *darling* is *Schatz,* literally, *something or someone valued highly.* In the Romance languages the words are the same. *Caro Mario,* I might address a letter to a friend, then let him know that I didn't buy the car I was looking at, after all, because it was *troppo caro, too dear.*

Contrite

Says the psalmist: "A humble and *contrite* heart, O Lord, you will not spurn" (see 33:19). What does the word mean? Is it related to *trite?*

The Latin original is the verb *conterere,* which means *to rub away,* with the prefix *con-* serving as an intensifier; *to rub away to dust. Contrition,* then, really does imply the sackcloth and ashes. The heart is trodden into the dust, ground away, rubbed to nothing. "The Lord is close to the broken hearted," says another of the psalms, and that may be because the Lord Himself has broken the heart in order to build it up again. Says George Herbert, in *The Altar:*

> *The heart alone*
> *Is such a stone*
> *As nothing but*
> *Thy power doth cut.*

The same idea of crushing and rubbing to dust is preserved in the word *trite.* Think of the *trite* phrase as linguistic rubble, the *detritus* of real thought. It is worn out, rubbed to nothing from too much handling. Another Latin word in the same clan is *tergere, to scrub,* from which we derive English *detergent,* and also something that's not really trite at all: the economic use of words, for rhetorical power: the *terse.*

Any relations in Germanic? Yes, but we have to imagine here the kind of rubbing away that happens on a lathe
or a potter's wheel. It's a circular rubbing, shaving, scraping. Grimm tells us that Latin *t* = Germanic *th*. Our word
in English is *throw*. If that seems strange, consider that if
you are going to throw a spear—or a football—you have
to impart a spin to it if you want it to go straight and not
wobble. Hence the German cousin of our *throw* is *drehen, to turn;* the surname *Dreher* is our *Turner,* the man
who works on a lathe. We turn spindles, in English, but
we don't turn clay pots. We *throw* a clay pot—not just at
the cat, but when we're making it on the wheel.

Our original word for throwing, though, was Anglo-
Saxon *weorpan* (cf. German *werfen*), which also had to
do with turning, and was related to a large group of Indo-
European words with *wr* in the root, whose ancient
sense was of turning or twisting (*wring, wrench, wrist,
wrinkle, writhe, wire*). One of those many words
might well be Latin *urbs*. We don't really know, but if
it is, the idea is that you can't have a city unless you
throw a wall up around it. The wall, not the throwing,
is implied by all the Germanic words that refer to a protected town: the *Burg;* hence the English *borough,* and
all those place-names like *Canterbury, Glastonbury,
Edinburgh, Peterborough,* and *Salisbury.*

thing

When my wife and I were first married, I cracked her up one evening reading aloud from Martin Heidegger about the "thingness of things." She was tired, and it didn't take much.

A *thing,* in its original Anglo-Saxon sense, wasn't just any old thing. A rock wasn't a thing. A pond wasn't a thing. That general sense—some inanimate object, or some abstract object of discussion—wasn't yet active. A *thing* was a gathering of men for the settling of household or public business. In Icelandic sagas, you're always waiting for the next *Thing* to come round, to adjudicate a boundary dispute, or to appeal to a fair arbiter for compensation to a man's family for burning his house down, say, with him in it. Then there was the big *Thing* once a year, when all the families of Iceland would convene: that was the *Althing: All-Thing.*

If that sounds funny, we might remember that the Romans had the same thing, er, idea. They called their thing the *res publica,* meaning the *public thing: the thing that has to do with the people as a people.* From that phrase they derived the single word *respublica,* our word *republic,* but by now the notion of a convening of people is almost wholly swallowed up by the charades of elections. A similar thing seems to have happened in the Romance languages, but not with Latin *res,* which was lost. Instead the word for a case at court, *causa,* a thing to be debated, came to denote any thingy thing at all: Italian *cosa,* French *chose.* When the Mafiosi called their organization *la cosa nostra, our "thing,"* they weren't necessarily being cagy. They meant, *our family affairs, our business.*

Sometimes the members of a large noble household would meet together for a *thing.* That was the *house-thing:* in Anglo-Saxon, *hus + thing > husting.* Yes, that's our word *hustings.* I always thought, when I was a kid, that *the hustings* that the politicians *hit*—because that's the only thing you do with hustings, you hit them—were like hurdles or short fences. I'm not sure where I got that idea, except that, now I think of it, it would be a good idea if we confined the hustings-hitters behind a very large fence. Then we might have some *thing* of our own again.

patriarch

En arche en ho Logos *(Jn 1:1).*

The word we translate as "beginning" had a richer range of meanings in ancient Greek. For us, "begin-ning" is temporal, or narrative, or sometimes spatial: the *beginning* of the American Republic, *Heere begin-nen the Tales of Caunterbury,* Route 33 *begins.* But when the Greek philosopher Thales suggested that water was the *arche* of the cosmos, he didn't mean that, once upon a time, there was nothing but water, and

now we have Athens, the poems of Homer, pomegranates, the moon, and Persians. He meant that, underlying the astounding variety of things in the world, there
was water. He meant that water was the foundation of
everything: the beginning, not in time, but in *being*.
The same sense flickers beneath the surface of the
Latin *principium,* which Saint Jerome used to translate *arche—principium,* not *inceptio.* The *principium*
is the beginning in the sense of the principle, the first-
head, we might say the fountainhead. It is more than
first in time; in John's Gospel, the *arche* or *principium*
is before time itself. It is first in the order of being.

Because it is ontologically first, it governs all things;
not as an arbitrary ruler from without, but as the ruling principle both from beyond and from within. To
describe brute political power, the Greeks preferred
forms of the verb *kratein, to wield power;* hence we
have *democracy, rule by the deme,* an artificial division of Athenian citizens established by the statesman
Cleisthenes to break the power of the *aristocracy, rule
by the aristoi,* the "best" citizens, not necessarily by
the richest citizens, which would have been a *plutoc-
racy.* What we have in America in theory is a *meri-
tocracy,* but in truth it is mere rule by rich ignorant
vicious snobs, who set themselves down like termites
and gnaw quietly away at the studs and rafters. Or it
is a *bureaucracy,* rule by people with all the life and
imagination of a file cabinet.

Therefore the *patriarch* is not a male boss, nor even
the father-boss. He is the *father-founder.* That, I think,
is what feminists object to most of all. It isn't that some
males are cads and thugs. Every good man knows this,
and every good man will strive to keep those miseries

in their place. It's that we should look for our root in the *Father:* the one whom Jesus called *Abba,* and Saint James called *the Father of Lights.* That would imply that a human family, well-led, with loving care and law extended to every member, might reflect, in a distant way, the patriarchy of the whole universe.

The name of the Blessed Mother is Hebrew *Mariam,* same as *Miriam,* possibly meaning *sea-light,* a lovely kenning for a star shining above the waters, or perhaps the moon gleaming serenely upon the waves. Hence the Latin calque *Stella Maris, Star of the Sea,* which then would denote *the star* to sail by, the star fixed in place, to guide us in the turmoil of life. So Shakespeare, on love: "It is the star to every wandering bark." Says Saint Bernard: "If the winds of temptation arise, if you are driven upon the rocks of tribulation, look to the star, call on Mary; if you are tossed upon the waves of pride, of ambition, of envy, of rivalry, look to the star, call on Mary."

We might be tempted to suppose that *Mariam* is related to the Latin *mare, sea;* after all, the Romans and other Indo-Europeans shared the same sea with the Hebrews, the Mediterranean, what the Romans would call, in their smug self-assurance, *Mare Nostrum, Our Lake.* It isn't, though. The first syllable in Mary's name would be the one that means *light.* Not light in its essence: that would be *'or*, what God created in the beginning when He said, *y'hi 'or, w'y'hi 'or, let there be light; and there was light*. But when God made the two great *lights*, the greater to rule the day and the lesser to rule the night, the word the sacred author uses is *mor* (*mar*).

Mariners called to Mary for her assistance upon the sea, but their occupation comes from the Latin *mare*. But what about good old English words? There's one, but we don't use it much. In the Pennsylvania countryside near where I grew up, there's a jewel of a lake where a glacier scooped out the top of a mountain. It is called Eagle's Mere. That's the word: *mere*. Not the adverb, as in *mere nonsense*. That's unrelated. It's the noun (cf. German *Meer, lake*). Pipes made of soft white clay are *meerschaum* pipes, from the German—literally, *sea-foam*, or, to make bad English of it, *mere-scum*.

I must admit here that this etymology of Mary's name was taken for granted by churchmen, but is much disputed. Another possibility is *bitter waters*, which would make the name a relative of the word for that bitter spice used to prepare a body for burial: *myrrh*.

But Mary—Maria, Marie—is a lovely name for a woman, quite aside from the implicit appeal to the one created being who sees, as Dante says, most profoundly into the divine. That name is not uttered in Dante's hell. Strange to say, it isn't common these days in the United States, either.

Clean

Our word is ancient, and has long embraced meanings both physical and spiritual. We still say of the rare politician that he has *clean hands,* or of the rare college football program that it has a *clean record.* If the word merely denoted an absence of the corrupt or squalid—no dirt—it wouldn't be so interesting. It would suggest what Milton called a sepulchral whiteness, a mere blank of virtue. But even now we sense that there's more to it than that.

That great Gawain-poet, the equal of his contemporary Chaucer, but whose name we do not know, wrote a long and vivid poem-homily on moral purity, called *Clannesse: Cleanness.* If you are a priest, he says, and you handle the holy things of God with a clean outside but an inside fouled with wickedness, you better watch out. You'll end up like the man who showed up at the wedding feast with his work clothes, torn and dirty, a sign of contempt for the feast, and not in holy-day apparel. "A clean heart create in me, O God, and renew a right spirit within me," says the psalmist. "Blessed are the pure in heart," says Jesus, and the phrase is sometimes rendered *clean of heart,* "for they shall see God." Cleanness suggests the brilliance of polished stone or glass; and in fact its ancient root in our common Indo-European tongue is a verb meaning "to shine." These include the many *gl-* words in English that have to do with light: *gleam, glimmer, glisten, glint, glow.* The Old English *claene* kept the ancient signification, but in other Germanic tongues the word swerved onto a different track, denoting what is neat, spiffy, just so, hence little: German *klein.*

There's a beloved Welsh song that celebrates a man of clean heart: *Calon Lan.* The adjective *glan* (softened to *lan* after a feminine noun; it's what Celtic adjectives beginning with certain consonants do) is related to our *clean* and to all those other bright words. But the Welsh also use *glan* where we use quite a different word. Now, the wonderful thing about poking around in another language is that you see how other people say things, sometimes because their languages have something yours doesn't, but sometimes because their languages *don't have something that your language does have,* and because of that very lack, they forge an association which you don't. That's the case with Welsh *glan.* When the angel tells Joseph in a dream that he is not to put Mary away, he reveals that the child within her has been begotten *o'r Yspryd Glan: by the Holy Spirit,* we say, but the Welshman says, *by the Clean Spirit.* And that should cause us to reconsider what cleanness and holiness have to do with one another. The Spirit's holiness is not a mere absence of sin, but a life-giving, abundant goodness, an overbrimming brilliance. True cleanness in man partakes of that fountain.

Most western European languages, outside of the Germanic sphere, use some form of Latin *liber* to denote the thing we read, and even we in English have our *libraries* for *book-lovers,* that is, *bibliophiles,* from the Greek *biblos, book.* Of course, from that Greek word we get our word for not just any old book, but The Book: *Bible.* So do the other languages: German *Bibel,* Italian *Bibbia,* French *Bible,* Welsh *Beibl.*

Anyway, wherever the Romans went, they brought their alphabet and their books and their word for their books, so that even a Celtic language like Welsh reflects that conquest: *llyfr, book.* But we Anglo-Saxons don't have that word. We have *book.* Where does that come from?

In old days, when people spent most of their time outside in good weather—basically, before the last generation or two—they knew a lot about the features of birds and animals, flowers and herbs, fruit and trees. They could tell the difference between an ash tree (hard wood, good for spears; hence poetic Anglo-Saxon *aesc* = *spear*) and a birch tree (much too soft for spears). They knew what the wood from various trees was good for.

Now there's a certain tree that is absolutely our best for two things: climbing and carving initials. It has big, smooth, muscle-like limbs that don't bend much under your feet. And because the bark is so smooth, even kind of glossy, you can carve initials in it that will be visible from far away and legible after forty or fifty years. It's the tree that the Romans called *fagus*. If we put that name through Grimm's Magic Metamorphoser, we remember that Latin *f* = Germanic *b*, and Latin *g* = Germanic *c / k*. The *fagus* is the Anglo-Saxon *bece*: German *Buche*, Modern English *beech*. Think of it then as the *book tree*. That's easier in German: *Buch* = book; *Buche* = beech (cf. the heinous camp at *Buchenwald: Beechwoods*).

Imagine etching "Tommy + Sally 4Ever" (or "4-eva" as they write it in Boston) on the bark of a beech tree. That's there for the duration. You've made an official record of it. You've *booked* it. Hence our odd word with the three consecutive pairs *bookkeeping* (double-entry bookkeeping was invented by bankers in the Middle Ages). Hence too what happens when you register an illegal wager on the Yankees: you *make book* with your *bookmaker*. You keep it up, and you'll hear Steve McGarrett, police commissioner, saying this to his right hand man: "*Book him*, Danno!"

When I was eight years old, I discovered baseball. I discovered it at the breakfast table, while reading the sports page. My father had the paper, across from me, and I read it upside down. The top team in the National League was the Saint Louis Cardinals, boasting four future Hall of Fame players: pitchers Bob Gibson and Steve Carlton, first baseman Orlando Cepeda, and left fielder Lou Brock.

For many years, the Cardinals' uniform has showcased the "birds on the bat," two redbirds perched atop a baseball bat, across the chest. The bird we call the *cardinal* is surely one of the most striking in the world; there isn't any bird like it in Europe. The male is bold red all over, with a jet-black mask and a perky crest; the female is gray tinged with the same bold red, and both have the bright yellow beak of the finch. That's what they are, finches—with strong seed-cracking beaks. They stay through the winter in most of eastern America, where they can be found searching for seeds and buds among the snow—a striking contrast. The male is a loud and gladsome singer, calling *what cheer cheer cheer* and *birdie birdie birdie birdie!*

The funny thing is that the team was not at first named for the bird. It was named for the color. Or rather it wasn't, until a lady fan remarked of the red trimming on the Saint Louis uniforms, "What a lovely shade of *cardinal!*" The name caught on, and eventually, management decided to illustrate the color by the bird.

So where does the color-word and the bird-name *cardinal* come from? Yes, from the *cardinals* of the Catholic Church. They wear red hats; in Italy, a man who has been raised to the cardinalate is designated by the descriptive participle *porporato: purpled!* But *purple*, for an Italian, is much closer to red than to violet. So the color comes from the hat and the robe. But the name *cardinal* comes from the role of those bishops; they are the ones who select the Pope, and they exercise authority over large dioceses. In other words, they are the *cardinal bishops,* the *bishops on whom a great deal hinges:* from Latin *cardo, cardinis: hinge.*

And the Lord God formed man out of the dust of the ground.

The word *Lord* in that sentence from Genesis translates the word *Adonai,* a substitute for the holy name of God, which the observant Jew will not utter aloud. The Jewish boy at his bar-mitzvah (the word means *son of the commandment*), will read aloud the ancient Hebrew blessing: *Baruch attah, Adonai Elohenu, Blessed are you, O Lord our God. Adonai* does not appear in the text, but the vowels for it do: Hebrew largely marks its vowels by "points," dots or lines placed above or beneath the previous consonant. So the vowels *a-o-a* appear in the points, though the consonants for the Name do not correspond with those vowels. That's the source of the misunderstanding that gives old texts the name "Jehovah," which really is a conflation of two completely different words.

The word for *Lord* really does vary from place to place and language to language, but the *anthropology* behind the word does not vary at all. In Old English, the *hlaford* is literally the *hlaf-weard, the loaf-warden,* the man who guards the loaves, the food supply. We lost the initial *h* and the medial *v* sound, leaving *lord*. In Latin, he's the *dominus,* literally the chief of the household, the *domus.* In the Romance languages, he's the eldest: *Il Signore sia con voi, Le Seigneur soit avec vous, The Lord be with you* (Italian, French). In German, he's *der Herr,* apparently originating in the idea that the chief will be gray haired; the same idea is present in Old English *gamolfeax, white-haired,* to describe a wise old ruler. In ancient Greek, he's *Kyrie,* from a root suggesting swelling, might, power. In Welsh, he's the *Arglwydd, Protector-Lord.*

A consistent picture emerges. A lord is a man who wields power; he is the chief of a people conceived as closely related, like a clan or family; he's old and wise; he is a protector. A bad ruler will therefore either throw his weight around, selfishly and willfully, or he will be weak and easily imposed upon; he will be foolish and juvenile; he will shirk his responsibilities. Our current politicians could learn a lot from old words.

"No one can call Jesus Lord, except by the Spirit," says Saint Paul (see 1 Cor 12:3). I have just looked at something called, ominously, *The New Century Hymnal,* in which the word *Lord* is avoided as if it were the carrier of a dreadful moral disease. It is Trinity Sunday as I write this, and I recall the first line of that mighty Trinitarian hymn: "Holy, holy, holy, Lord God almighty!" The editors of this hymnal won't have any of it. "God the almighty," they say, to avoid acknowledging Him as Lord. We should rather think it our greatest honor to be *permitted* to call Him Lord.

Our word today is from the ancient Greek, but it didn't mean people whose minds were very slow. Ol' Polyphemus, in the *Odyssey*, was an *idiot*, but not because of the one big eye in the middle of his forehead, or because of his sloppy table manners. The Cyclops was an idiot, in the Greek eye, because he didn't do what civilized men would do. He had a great island for planting grain and grapes and olives, but he didn't do any of that. He and his fellow Cyclopses never assembled peaceably to pursue the common good; they had no town meetings. "Every family ignored its neighbors," says Homer, who evidently stepped into a time machine to visit any one of your typical American suburbs of the twenty-first century.

The word *idiot* denoted the antithesis to someone living in a free, self-governing *polis:* the man who is worthless for such liberty. He's all about himself and no one else. *That* is the essence of the word. If your argument against some measure of morality is a version, however dressed up in sophisticated language, of "Duh, yew can't tell ME what ta do, duh," you are an idiot. By this definition, all relativists are idiots. Doctrinaire libertarians are idiots. Sexual revolutionaries are idiots. People who say they believe in God but won't go near "organized religion" (while they fall prone before mass education, mass entertainment, and mass politics) are idiots.

Do we have other words that are related? There's Welsh *eiddo, (one's) own;* but mainly we have words from the Greek that have not attracted the sense of mental deficiency. Thus someone with an *idiosyncrasy* has a habit peculiar to himself; it's not just that he bites his fingernails, which lots of people do, but that he bites them in public, then makes a show of spitting them out. That would be so odd as to constitute an *idiosyncrasy:* like Stan Musial's unique peekaboo batting stance, or Van Gogh's big woolly stars. Sometimes an idiosyncrasy is pleasant or comical; more often it's just a little bit annoying.

My favorite related word, though, is *idiolect.* No, that is not the special speech of politicians. That is denoted by the technical term *gibberish.* Nor is it the language of bureaucrats, educationists, and people who parrot their pronouncements: that is *jargon, argot, patois.* It is not the language of a reasonably well-defined sub-group, like the people who live on the Orkney Islands: theirs is a *dialect.* Nor the words and sayings and lin-guistic constructions of people who share a social class (*patois*), or a line of work (*argot, jargon*). An *idiolect* is a form of the language peculiar to one person alone. He goes beyond the *idiom* of his neighbors, and says things that only he says, or that only he says in the way that he says them. It is likely, for instance, that only Yukon Cornelius calls the Abominable Snowman of the North by the tumbly-humbly name of "bumble." And he cer-tainly knows one of the idiosyncrasies of the bumble. "Bumbles bounce!"

heart

I've heard it said that people in old days believed that we thought with our hearts rather than with our brains. That actually seems to be a silly legend, like the belief that people before Columbus believed that the earth was flat (no, they knew it was round). People before Copernicus, most of them, believed that the sun traveled around the earth, whereas we know now that the world revolves around the desires of middle and upper class western European and American women.

Anyway, our Old English *heorta* is cognate with Latin **cord* (*cor, cordis*), and Greek *kardia;* Grimm's Law, we recall, associates Germanic *h* with Greek and Latin *c (k)*. Welsh, which lies with the Celtic languages on the Greco-Roman side, has *calon*. The *heart* is naturally associated with emotions, since, as we know, it sure does beat more strongly when we are excited, or afraid, or exuberant, or in love (which last state may well imply the other three). It is also taken figuratively as the center of everything. "The heart has reasons which the mind knows nothing of," said Pascal, and of course he wasn't referring to the organ that pumps blood—or not merely that. He was referring to the deep center of the whole human being, to things that transcend discursive reasoning. It is why Jesus, citing Scripture, says, "You shall love the Lord your God with all your heart and mind and strength and soul" (see Mk 12:30). We might ask, too, what our wives might say if we told them that we loved them with all our minds, but not with all our heart. Ain't the mind more important than the heart? I don't believe they would like that.

"Heart of Jesus, pierced with a lance," we pray in the Catholic litany of the Sacred Heart, "have mercy on us." We'd do well to consider why we know exactly what that means, even though we are called on to consider that heart, in the center of His body, pierced, after He had died. We do have another word in English that clarifies what that heart is. It's from Old French, through those Norman invaders we've met many times before. It came from their word for *heart: coeur.* That is our word *core:* what is at the heart of our beings.

That's where you go to get your poisons. In fact, the Greek word *pharmakon,* from which we derive, through Medieval Latin and French, our word *pharmacy,* meant a drug, or a poison, or a potion, or a spell, or all of them at once. It's easy to see why. Most drugs are poisons. We take them in large enough quantities to kill the disease, but not large enough to kill us. In this sense there's no difference between radiation therapy, chemotherapy, and penicillin. Or we take something that is generally harmful, even deadly, for a healthy person, but in certain cases the only thing that can heal the sick; so a

man having a heart attack may take digitalis, distilled
from the foxglove, but if he's not having a heart attack
and he takes it, it may well be his last act on earth.

C. S. Lewis once wrote that the difference between
modern science and old-fashioned demon worship was
that the former was effective, and the latter was generally not. That is, both have as their aims the human
domination of nature—power. Perhaps that explains the
sinister associations we still have with the word *drug,*
and the sinister associations that the word *pharmakon*
used to have. For it is in the Bible, that word. It appears,
among other places, in the Apocalypse of John, and is
translated in the King James Bible as *sorceries.* If we
set aside the ingredients of the brew, and look at the
motive, we can glimpse the perennial human fascination with control—casting spells, or pumping somebody with psychoactive drugs, or extorting submission
from them by a combination of threat and glamour. The
pharmakon is what the whore of Babylon is drinking,
inebriated with wealth and power.

It explains too why, in the *Quest of the Holy Grail,*
the good Sir Galahad comes not to bring magic, but
to dispel it, to rid the kingdom of Logres from the
enchantments to which it is subject. Those are, shall
we say, the incantations of evil. It's interesting that the
word *enchantment,* like the word *magic,* has followed
the track onward and upward, so that you can hardly
expect a tourist brochure to allure you if it doesn't blare
about the magic or the enchantment of this riviera or
that casino. "Let me drug you," says the sexy adver-
tisement in the magazine, as you are waiting for your
prescription to be filled at the pharmacy. "You do want
to fall under my power, don't you? Because I can give

you power. I can make you young again! I can give you a chiseled body! I can deliver hot lovemaking," and perhaps they can, if we remember what lower place they got it from.

"Sweets for the sweet," says Queen Gertrude sadly, as she tosses flowers into the open grave of Ophelia. The phrase has entered our language, as something you'd say to your best girl on Valentine's Day, when you give her a box of fancy chocolates. Or at least you used to do that, till the Lonely Revolution. Now you can go listen to angry spoiled college girls shouting obscenities. "You catch more flies with honey than with vinegar," my father used to say, but he hadn't reckoned on an open sewer.

The word was a favorite of Chaucer's, which he used to describe the beauty of youth (even the rascally youth Nicholas in *The Miller's Tale*), or of a melody, or of persuasive words. "Heard melodies are sweet, but those unheard / Are sweeter," says Keats in his famous *Ode on a Grecian Urn*, as he beholds the urn's relief sculpture of youth and love. When the lovely Beatrice first appears to Virgil, to urge him to go to the assistance of the lost wanderer Dante, her words are sweet, *soave*—what becomes our word *suave*, meaning for us something a good deal less than sweet. George Herbert builds a whole poem around the word:

Sweet day, so cool, so calm, so bright,
The bridal of the earth and sky:
The dew shall weep thy fall tonight,
    For thou shalt die.

Sweet rose, whose hue, angry and brave,
Bids the rash gazer wipe his eye:
Thy root is ever in its grave,
    For thou must die.

Sweet spring, full of sweet days and roses,
A box where sweets compacted lie;
My music shows ye have your closes,
    And all must die.

Only a sweet and virtuous soul,
Like seasoned timber, never gives,
But though the whole world turn to coal,
    Then chiefly lives.
                    —*Virtue,* George Herbert

A brilliant poem; the sweetnesses of all this world, made sweeter or bittersweet by our knowing that they must pass away, is as nothing compared with the sweetness of a soul grown mature in virtue, a "seasoned" soul, like good sound timber, like the sound wood of the Tree of Life, the only thing that remains sweet and whole after the world is reduced to dust.

The word, then, is really quite rich. Its relations in other languages bear this out. In Latin, *suavis* suggests something easy, pleasant, gentle—literally, when you *persuade* somebody, you *sweet-talk* him. Homer says that the Muses dash the words of the wise man with honey, with grace, that he may win the hearts of the people to do what is right. "Taste and see that the Lord is sweet," says the Psalmist. He isn't talking about a mere lingual perception, but of an entire experience of beauty. In this sense, *sweet* is the opposite of *sour,* if the latter word is taken to describe not the taste of certain cheeses, but a moral curdling, a corruption; and the opposite of *bitter,* if that word describes the harshness of suffering, or of evil. That is why the children of Israel remembered the waters of Meribah, the waters of bitterness, where they tempted the Lord in the desert.

Perhaps even before we judge the moral character of a civilization, we might judge its sweetness—or its bitterness. Nowadays even our laughs are harsh and ring hollow. Maybe that is because we pursue sweetness in the wrong places, or pursue it for pleasure's sake alone. That is the curdling result of *hedonism:* from a distant cousin of *sweet,* in ancient Greek: *hedone, pleasure.*

Reading from the dictionary: *irony.* n. 1. That feature of wit least likely to be found in an academic essay.

Aristotle called *eironeia* the habit of not-quite-honest self-deprecation, as when Socrates used to go around Athens insisting that he didn't know anything. So its basic definition, the one that a stranger will blurt out if you collar him on the street corner and demand it, is that you're ironic when you say the opposite of what you mean.

But I've always found that definition to be woefully inadequate. My test case is the professor and the banana peel. Suppose you are walking down the street with a professorial sort who is holding forth on the nature of irony. He is boring you to tears, but you're not saying a word. Right in front of him is a banana peel. You see him, you see the peel, but you don't say a thing. And just when he launches into the linguistic heights, slllllip—thud! And you smile. Ironic, isn't it? And yet you haven't said a word.

We need a definition that will cover all of what we call ironic, and, years ago, I came up with one that I still think does the trick. Irony involves the revelation of a clash between knowledge and ignorance, or between one level of knowledge and a deeper level of knowledge. Anybody can say, with a smirk and a toss of the head, "Well, I hope so!"—meaning, "That will never happen while I have anything to do with it, you bounder!" That is ironic, but it isn't artful. The real ironist is always an artist, and seeks not to conceal but to reveal by surprise: to enlist your attention by making you either an actor in a dramatic scene or a deeply interested spectator.

The greatest example of irony in Scripture—I owe this insight to a brilliant colleague of mine at Providence College—comes when the prophet Nathan appears unannounced before King David, who has committed adultery with Bathsheba and then arranged to have her husband Uriah, a Hittite who serves most faithfully both God and his king, slaughtered in the front lines of battle. Nathan proceeds to speak about a rich man who owned large flocks. When a visitor came to him, he did not take from his own, but seized the only lamb of his poor neighbor, who loved the animal as if it were a daughter. Then the rich man slew it for the table.

"As the Lord is my witness," cries King David, "that man shall die!"

"*You* are that man," says Nathan (see 2 Sam 12:5–6).

See how it works? The parable brings us into the evil of David's deed; we know that he has done a wicked thing, and we begin to see the parallel between that and the wickedness of the man in the story. We also see that David knows what is right, even though he does not know that Nathan knows the evil he has done. We see him convicted by his own words. The simple statement by Nathan, "You are that man," surprises him into terrible self-knowledge. He thought he knew everything; he thought he had kept his crime secret. He is shown to have known little indeed.

That is ironic. But then, ironies do abound in Scripture. How could they not? "For my ways are not your ways, nor are my thoughts your thoughts," says the Lord.

resurrection

I write this on Easter Sunday, having celebrated with my family the resurrection of Jesus from the dead. A few years ago I heard a television anchorman say that

Easter was when Christians celebrate the day that Jesus rose into heaven; which is a little like saying that on the Fourth of July, Americans celebrate Washington's victory at Yorktown. Only a little, though, because on that Easter morning we are set free from the bondage of sin and death, if we wish for that freedom; the victory is complete. Christ rose not to heaven but *from the grave,* to walk with His disciples again and speak to them, even to eat with them, before He returned to the right hand of the Father.

Our word that describes the most important event in human history, in some ways the only important event, comes from the Latin *resurgo, resurgere, resurrexi, resurrectus.* It has three parts to it, two of them somewhat obscured by combination. The prefix *re-* suggests a return to an original state, going back again, so someone who *revives* does not have a second life exactly, but returns to the first life. Someone who is *resuscitated* is, literally, roused up again, to resume the former healthy breathing. Neither of these verbs means what the Christian means by *resurrection.*

We draw closer to the heart of the matter when we consider the other two elements. One is an adverb, the other a verb. The adverbial prefix *sur-,* whose equivalent we do not have in English, means *up from below:* so the Latin command in the Mass, *sursum corda,* means, with the verb left implicit, *hearts up from below,* that is, *lift up your hearts.* When we *surmount* a difficulty we overcome it against the odds, from below. The verbal element is *regere: to direct, to be straight.* If we put all three together, the entire verb suggests a rising again upright from below: it implies Christ's descent into death and the netherworld.

"My dear," says the saleslady, spreading out the filigree dress, woven from 20 percent silk, 20 percent cotton, 20 percent spandex, and 40 percent air, "you'll be the *envy* of every girl at the prom!"

"I'll say! But can you really put it on without tearing it?"

"Sure, no problem. Just don't laugh too hard!"

The saleslady does not say, "Young lady, you shall be the cause of a profound spiritual evil in those who look upon you at the dance." She wants her sale, after all, and *envy*, like *pride*, has had a semantic face lift in the last century, much of the cost of the operation defrayed by advertisers, who find that the deadly sins are more useful than the virtues for parting the fool from his money.

The word *envy* comes to us through French, but its Latin form, *invidia*, reveals the inner perversity of the sin. It is, literally, *in-vidia*, an *inside-out seeing*. English preserves much the same idea in a similar word: to look at someone *cross-eyed* is to look with enmity, usually unwarranted, so that we suspect that the trouble lies in the beholder rather than in the one he beholds. The theologians define envy as a willful sorrow in response to someone else's good—and the sin is perfectly demonic if the good in question is spiritual. "Young love," says the divorcee, sucking one last draw on her Marlboro before crushing it out on the china, "I know what *that's* all about. They'll learn better soon enough," she says, enjoying their disillusionment in anticipation.

Milton illustrates for us most powerfully, almost comically, what the sin is and what the word means. Satan, like a voyeur, is spying upon the naked Adam and Eve. They two, young people in love, surrounded by Paradise, perfectly naked and innocent and alone and endowed with astonishing beauty, hold hands and talk about when they first met—for some things have blessedly not changed since those lost days in Eden. But the conversation comes to an end, and then it is time for kissing. We too, we who are no longer innocent, see the ravishing scene from an uneasy point of view:

> *So spake our general Mother, and with eyes*
> *Of conjugal attraction unreproved*
> *And meek surrender, half embracing leaned*
> *On our first Father, half her naked breast*
> *Swelling met his under the flowing gold*
> *Of her loose tresses hid.*

At which point I hear female despisers of marriage scoffing and snarling, "What is this *meek surrender!* How disgraceful," knowing in their hearts how dearly they would love such a man as Adam to surrender to, if he could find them as lovely as Adam finds Eve. Their reaction is like that of the third party to this scene:

> *Aside the devil turned*
> *For envy, and with jealous leer malign*
> *Eyed them askance, and to himself thus plained:*
> *"Sight hateful, sight tormenting! Thus these two,*

Emparadised in one another's arms,
The happier Eden, shall enjoy their fill
Of bliss on bliss, while I to Hell am thrust,
Where neither joy nor bliss, but fierce desire,
Among our other torments not the least,
Still unfulfilled with pain of longing pines . . ."

No wonder he looks at them out of the side of his eye. Beauty, joy, innocence, peace, godliness, and honor are magnetic. They command our attention; Satan cannot help but look. Read that great poem, and note how often the enemy writhes in the twists of just such self-hating, agonizing envy.

In the Beetle Bailey comic strip, the old addled General Halftrack has a dumb blonde secretary with really dangerous curves. Her name, of course, is Miss *Buxley.* Mort Walker was punning on the word *buxom,* which is now used only to describe a woman—and not every woman, either!

It wasn't always so. In *Paradise Lost,* Milton describes Satan as flying through the *buxom air.* What could he have meant? Was the air a blonde?

We need to return to the Old English: *bugsam.* The second part of the word is our suffix *some:* winsome, lonesome, handsome; it is the same suffix as the German *-sam: langsam.* It suggests that something is really characterized by what precedes: it's the real deal. So what did the *bug-* mean? Was something *bugsam* full of bugs?

No. The Old English verb *bugan* meant *to bend.* The old g's at the ends of syllables often turned, by Middle English, into the semivowels *w* and *y,* so we have quite a few words in English that have to do with bending, that have those sounds at the end of a little word beginning with b: *bow* (both kinds), *bough, bay, bight.* Some people call a *bay* window a *bow* window: the idea is the same. German had many of the same words, so we end up with Yiddish *bagel.* Bagels have bends in them.

So something that is *buxom* is pliant, yielding—it gives way, it bends. But I trust Miss Buxley didn't.

Sometimes a thing bends because it is weak. So Shakespeare says that true love does not *bend with the remover to remove.* Or we say of someone who is suffering that he is *bowed low* by adversity. But a stubborn man *will not bend,* and a proud man *will not bow.* Such as the latter, so common in our day, do not realize that it is an honor to *bow* the head and *bend* the knee before the Lord.

The bureaucrats who turned the English Mass into kindergarten talk, back in the early 1970's, went into asthmatic spasms every time they encountered a formal synonym for such verbs as *ask* and *pray.* You can say, in a dumbed-down reader for little children, "See Jane pray. Pray, Jane, pray!" But you could never say, "See Dan beseech. Beseech, Dan, beseech!" So that word had to go. Along with it went plenty of other words with all of their various shades of meaning: *beg, invoke, entreat, plead, cry, supplicate.*

The idea was to scrub away any trace of a language that was heard as sacred. It was why the same demolition team often translated Latin *sanctus* as . . . nothing. They just left it out. They left a lot of things out, or rather ripped a lot of things out. Beware of people who reduce. If you go to a Congregationalist church, look to the figures in the windows: there aren't any. Look to the evidence that sacraments are administered: there won't be any evidence. That was the ideal the demolition team had in mind, a linguistic blank.

Anyway, English *beseech* survived for a long time mainly in poetry and in prayers. It is not a hard word to understand, because as soon as you have heard the phrase "we *beseech* thee" two or three times, you get the idea, even if you still play hopscotch and jump rope. The word itself is made of two parts, the *be* and the *seech*. The first is a prefix that turns our attention strongly towards the beneficiary or the sufferer of the action that we are naming: you *bespatter* someone with paint; you *bedeck* the stage with flowers. Here, we *seek* something precious to us, and that is why we *beseech* God when we pray for it. We might say that we press our seeking upon God. Our verb should be **seech,* not *seek,* but the latter form came into the language through the Norse, who settled in parts of England during the tenth and eleventh centuries. In Norse, the *c (k)* sound did *not* turn into *ch* in the vicinity of the vowels *ae, e, i.* So we end up with quite a few Anglo-Saxon / Norse doublets: *ditch, dike; shirt, skirt.* If we were consistent, we would have *seech, beseech,* from the Anglo-Saxon, or the forms *seek, beseek,* from the Norse.

The past tense is *besought* (cf. *seek, sought;* like *bring, brought; teach, taught*). That is not because the past is irregular. It is because the *present* is irregular. That is, the past is original, but something happened to change the present. The original verb was Anglo-Saxon *socjan* (pronounced *SOHK-yahn*), *seek,* with past tense *sohte, sought.* The *j* in the present stem altered the preceding vowel, moving it to the front for ease of pronunciation; then the *j* disappeared, leaving us with a present *secan, seek.* The same thing happened and left us with the "new" verbs *tell* and *sell,* with their past tenses, which are original: *told, sold.*

"Hey Matty, hey Matty," said the football player down the hall to his groggy roommate, "what's all this *beeah* on the *flooah?*" I was a freshman at Princeton, and it was the first time I ever heard a Rhode Island accent in all its glory.

We don't know where the word *beer* comes from. We think we know where the stuff itself comes from: ancient Mesopotamia. Think about it. Would you really want to drink the runoff in the canals and standing pools from the sluggish Tigris and Euphrates? The beer was clean.

And, like wine, it gladdened the heart, back in the days
before people drove cars too fast and gladdened the vul-
tures. I'm told that it was thick foamy stuff which people
would drink through reeds from a common tub. Some
things never change!

The word was *beor* in Anglo-Saxon, but my favorite form of it comes from Bede's history of the English
church: *gebeorscip, beership, feast,* pronounced
ye-BEH-or-ship. That's what the men were having in
one of the out-buildings at the abbey at Whitby, and you
can't have a party with Germans unless there are two
things: *beor* and poetry. Imagine a group of Germanic
cowherds and plowmen sitting at a big oak table, drinking beer and banging their mugs, shouting, "Po-em, poem!" Well, that wasn't the word, but you get the idea.
And they'd pass the harp around—not the big stringed
thing, but a sort of zither—and the men would sing
heroic poems of the great pagan warriors of old, like
Sigemund and Beowulf. But Caedmon left the beership,
because he didn't know any songs, he said; or maybe
he had some uneasiness in his conscience about them.

It was his turn that night to settle the cows in their
stalls, so he did that, and fell asleep, when an angel of
the Lord appeared to him in a dream and said, in Anglo-
Saxon, "Caedmon, sing me something."

"But I don't know anything to sing—and that's why I
left the beership."

"Still, you can sing."

"What shall I sing?"

"*Sing me frumsceaft*—sing for me the First-Making."

And so began the venerable tradition of Christian
poetry in the heroic meter and idiom of Anglo-Saxon.

Caedmon was so startled by it all, he told the story to his boss the bailiff the next morning. The bailiff knew that divine inspiration was beyond his pay, so he brought Caedmon to the abbess, Saint Hilda. She said to the monks, "This may be from God," and asked them to read to Caedmon one of the stories from Scripture, so that he could go home with it in his mind, and compose a poem from it. If he could do that, then surely they were encountering something miraculous. They did, and Caedmon did, and he ended up joining the monastery itself, never learning to read or write, but composing poem after poem of great power and spiritual insight, and becoming the most beloved of brothers.

But if Caedmon had hung around and drunk the beer, who knows? We might have ended up with silly beer jingles instead, like this one, from *I Love Lucy*:

> *"Lots of ale and stout are on my shelf,*
> *And I take a drop or two myself!"*
> *"A drop, he says—the Squire's got the gout,*
> *The stout makes him ail and the ale makes him*
>   *stout!"*

One of my favorite quips of all time, by Dorothy Parker, on the acting talents of Katharine Hepburn: "They run the gamut from A to B." (Frankly, I don't care for her acting either, except in screwball comedies or *The African Queen;* the unrelated Audrey is the superior Hepburn, and prettier too.) It's right there with another quip of hers, when a man jestingly allowed her to precede him through a doorway, saying, "Age before beauty." "Pearls before swine," said Dorothy Parker.

What's a *gamut,* anyhow? Is it a string of catgut? A haunch of pork? A bazaar table filled with overpriced shawls? A Turkish cigar? A review of kilt-clad Scotsmen on a windy day? What is it?

It's a musical scale, that's what it is: a *gamma-ut,* from *gamma* (the Greek letter to signify the G, the note below A) and *ut,* which we now call *do,* as in the amiable Rogers and Hammerstein folly, as Austrian children sing out with British accents, and jump up and down the steps at a park in Salzburg:

Do, a deeah, a female deeah,
Re, a drop of golden sun . . .

The monks in the Middle Ages, when they were not preserving civilization, draining swamps and turning them into arable land, inventing technology to increase the yield of farms, and praying, gave to the world what we now hear as the eight note scale. Guido of Arezzo is credited with inventing musical notation, naming his notes according to the syllables of a famous hymn in honor of John the Baptist:

UT *queant laxis* REsonare *fibris*
MIra *gestorum* FAmuli *tuorum,*
SOLve *polluti* LAbii *reatum,*
  Sancte Joannes.

That your servants may resound
With loosened cords your wondrous deeds,
Cleanse away the blame of soiled lips,
     O holy John.

Do you see the progression? Do, re, mi, fa, sol, la . . . where's ti? Well, they hadn't invented it quite yet, but it soon came, along with that most brilliant of innovations, B flat, followed by the other black notes on the piano, till we now have our full twelve tone scale.

Veni, creator Spiritus,
mentes tuorum visita,
imple superna gratia,
quae tu creasti pectora.

Come, Holy Ghost, Creator blest,
And in our hearts take up Thy rest;
Come with Thy grace and heavenly aid
To fill the hearts which Thou hast made.
                    —Rabanus Maurus, 9ᵗʰ century

The word *spirit* comes to us straight from Latin *spiritus,* which does not in the first instance mean something like a ghost or a specter. It is a verbal noun: *a breathing.* We mustn't think of the Spirit of God as a vague remainder after God has departed for somewhere else, not only because God fills every infinitesimal quantum of being with his immensity, but also because the Spirit is by very definition *active:* it is the *breath* of God, breathing existence itself into all things. The idea is similar to that which gave us the word *energy,* a Greek word adopted into Latin first by the theologians, to describe the action of the Holy Spirit within the human heart. It's an *in-working* (English *work,* cousins with Latin *urgere, to drive,* and Greek *ergon, work,* with the ancient initial *w* lost). Then *energia* was taken up by men of letters to describe the instilled power of a work of art. Only rather recently did the physicists adopt it.

In the history of the English word, we can draw two tracks from the Latin *spiritus,* one labeled "specter" and one labeled "energy." The first track is a lonesome one. It will describe something "in the air"—notice the similar metaphor—like a *spirit* of hope, or a *spirit* of despair, or Mr. Spock's *spirit,* somehow impressed into the brains of Dr. McCoy by carpal-cranial contact. The second track is more gregarious. It gives us *spirits,* as in bourbon and brandy. It blows the trumpet for *school spirit,* which means that youngsters jump up and down when Fats McAlister bowls over Mayfield's linemen for a touchdown. It gives us the backslapping boss who bellows, "That's the *spirit!*" when we agree under duress to work all day on Saturday.

Neither *spirit* comes close to the mysterious meaning of Hebrew *ruah* or Greek *pneuma* or Latin *spiritus,* when the Spirit of God was hovering above the waters of creation, or when the Spirit descended upon (and into!) the apostles in the upper room, and they were *inspired,* given words they had not known how to speak before.

A Grammatical Interlude:

Like as the waves move to the pebbled shore,
So do our minutes hasten to their end.
> —Shakespeare

And as a tower clock that tolls the hour
    when the Bride of the Lord rises to sing
    morningsong to her Spouse, to win His love,
Sounding so sweet a knelling of ting ting
    as all the gears within it push and pull,
    a soul that's well disposed must hear the ring
And swell with love: so now I heard that wheel
    rendering voice to voice in harmony,
    and with such sweetness as no man can feel
If not where joy is for eternity.
> —Dante

The usual definition of a *simile* is that it's a compar-ison that uses *like* or *as*, while a metaphor is a com-parison that doesn't. But how helpful is that? What is so important about a couple of little words? Are we drawing a distinction without a difference? Why should we have two words to describe what is essentially one thing?

The problem is that similes in English usually employ those words, not because there's anything decisive about those words, but because the *nature of a simile* leads us almost inevitably to use them. The words are like snapped twigs, little signs that the simile beast may be lurking about, ready to rush us with his tusks.

It's best, I think, to define the simile as an extended comparison or analogy, with specific elements in the object of the simile corresponding with specific elements in the *vehicle* of the simile—the wagon that delivers the object. The simile is thus a kind of compressed parable. Let's look at the similes above. You're standing at a seashore, and you watch the waves coming in, one after another, never ceasing, breaking upon the pebbly beach and then vanishing in foam. Such are our minutes. They arrive from the mystery of the future, one after another, never ceasing, breaking upon the present moment, and then vanishing forever. The simile is apt—that is, it does fit what we are talking about, it reveals something otherwise obscure in our experience of time. It brings that truth before our eyes so powerfully that it will be hard for the lover of Shakespeare to stand upon a beach on a quiet day and not think about time, and how fast it comes and goes.

Or look at Dante's more elaborate simile, comparing the joyous singing and dancing of souls in Purgatory with the ordered and various motions of the wheels and gears in a clock—and not just any clock, but one upon a tower that tolls and summons the Church to rise to sing matins to Christ, in a dawn-song of love. How does this simile work? The souls are in union with one another, but each one is distinct, each is a fully realized personality. They are thus like the whirring and turning elements in the works of a clock, some slow, some fast, some moving this way, some moving that way, but the whole, the community, is ordered to one object, the tolling of the hour. And what is that, here? Just as a bride awakes in the morning to sing a love song to her beloved bridegroom, so the Church awakes in the morning, and for these souls it is a morning that never fades, to sing to Christ.

The epic poets Homer and Virgil were masters of the simile, knowing both how to construct them and, what is almost as important, when to use them. That's because the reader will tire of them quickly, especially if he senses that they are tossed in only for poetic fireworks. Be sparing in their use!

remember

It is an old word for a mysterious thing, one whose essence Augustine pondered in his *Confessions*. What does it mean, not just to think, or imagine, but to *remember?* When the Ghost of Hamlet Senior says to Hamlet Junior, *Remember me,* what does he mean? Does he simply mean, "Don't forget me?" Does my dog Jasper *remember* things, in that sense? When we go to visit our kinfolk in Pennsylvania, he must smell the slate in the very hills, or the fish and weeds in the Delaware

River, because when we draw near he grows antsy and starts to whine. He knows!

So, yes, in that sense he does remember; a sight or sound or smell comes to him, and he knows, "That's my master," or "That's the cute German shepherd from around the corner," or at least he knows it in a doggish kind of way. But he doesn't set about remembering. That doesn't just mean that he can't memorize. He doesn't make his own mind an object of his mind; he doesn't set his mind to direct his thinking.

When we *remember,* in Hamlet's sense, or on Memorial Day, or when we follow the commandment of Christ, "Do this in remembrance of me," we deliberately hold something in mind or bring it back to mind. We treasure it, like the Psalmist on his bed, meditating upon the great gift of the Law. The word reflects the reality. That *b* in there doesn't belong; it's a parasite that developed after the *m,* in Old French: press your lips together, make a humming sound, then shut it off abruptly, and you can hear how that happened. *Remember* is related to Latin *memor, mindful of;* cf. French *memoire,* Italian *memoria,* English *memory.* It suggests that something dwells securely in the *mens,* the *mind.* (The same hardening of *m* to *mb* gives us English *number,* from Latin *numerus,* and *humble,* Latin *humilis*).

English speakers developed a useful verb from that noun: *mind.* To *mind your business* means, in the first instance, to set your *mind* to *your business,* like *minding the store.* It means to remember your duty. Your grandmother might have said to you, if you were misbehaving, "Mind me, now." If we *don't mind* what somebody is apologizing for, we mean that it won't stay in our minds; it's there and gone.

But some things we should *mind*. On Memorial Day, we remember those men who minded the business of the nation, fighting against her enemies in wars foreign and domestic, and laying down their lives. Only human beings *remember*, in this sense; and when a culture ceases to remember, it ceases to be a culture, and ceases to be fully human.

"Except a *corn* of wheat fall into the ground and die," says Jesus, in the King James version, "it abideth alone; but if it die, it bringeth forth much fruit" (Jn 12:24). That is the headnote to Fyodor Dostoyevsky's *The Brothers Karamazov*, in my opinion the greatest novel ever written. The highly compressed parable begs us to consider the miraculous transformation of the corn of wheat, the seed, which is only potentially alive until it ceases to be itself—until it falls into the ground and dies; and then it attains its fulfillment in fruit. The analogy of the seed with selfish, half-blind, worldly man is rich also. One cannot come to an end of contemplating it. We cannot come to life unless we die. "He who would save his life must lose it," says Jesus.

But why is it *corn*, and not *grain*? Well, that's because *corn* is the older word, original in English, to describe one of the grains of those wonderful grasses that give us bread or meal: wheat, barley, rye, oats. It's the Old English cousin of Latin *granum, grain*: recall that Latin *g* = Germanic *c (k)*. The word *grain,* like many of our monosyllabic words using the digraph *ai* (*main, plain, aid, frail, train, bail;* but not *rain, sail, laid, wail, braid*), comes to us through the French, after the Norman Conquest. So began the bitter competition between *corn* and *grain,* locked in wrestling holds, each trying to throw the other and either drive it from the language or limit it to some petty specialized meaning. Hence we have *corn* as uppermost in the King James Bible, with *grain* usually demoted to referring to something *like* a corn: a *grain* of sand. Hence *grain* becomes a unit of that Frenchy *avoirdupois (have-of-the-weight)* weight system.

But *grain,* on the winnowing floor, just when *corn* was a-raising his arms in triumph, shot out a leg and tripped that boaster, and scrambled on top, though not decisively: *grain* came to refer not only to things that look like grains, but to the seeds themselves, while *corn* still referred to the fruit, that is, the wheat, barley, rye, and oats. And then came the Mayflower, and that bleak day for *corn,* when the Indians at Plymouth showed William Bradford and his fellow settlers the fruit called maize, native to the Americas. It was the only *grain* these Indians cultivated. So the Pilgrims just called it *grain,* that is, *corn,* or *Indian corn;* and that explains why in the United States that yellow stuff on the cob that tastes so sweet with butter and salt and gets between your teeth is called *corn,* that and that alone, while *grain* refers to everything else.

Then things for *corn* went from bad to worse. What's something that only *hayseeds* would enjoy, rather than pinch-nosed urban sophisticates? Something *corn-pone,* that's what. And what about a joke that makes you roll your eyes, because you know it's coming, and because it's got that sweet sentimentality about it, and so it sticks between your teeth? It's *corny*, what else? And if you hit a lazy pop fly to the outfield, it's a *can of corn;* I don't know why.

And what about those hard painful nubs on the sides of your toes, that swell and throb when the rain's coming? Those are your *corns.* Your grains, your seeds? No, not in this case. These *corns* have nothing to do with *corn.* They are your *cornus,* neuter plural, from Latin *cornu:* Germanic *horn.*

pomegranate

One of Botticelli's masterpieces is the *Madonna della Granata,* the *Madonna of the Pomegranate.* It's a glorious enamel painting in the round, with a solemn Mary surrounded by angels in the form of Italian lads, holding in her arms the baby Jesus, who is picking one of the edible seeds from a pomegranate. That's a clever allusion to classical mythology and to Scripture. Proserpina, the lovely daughter of the grain goddess Ceres (in Greek, *Demeter = Ge-meter, earth mother*), was dragged off to the underworld by Pluto. So long as Proserpina refused to eat anything down under, she could return to the earth without any harm done, but she grew hungry, and ate six pomegranate seeds. That is why, for six months of the year, the earth does not give forth its *cereal* bounty, because Ceres is distracted, mourning for her daughter. But for the other six months, Proserpina returns above, and Ceres rejoices, and flowers spring forth, and trees bear fruit, including pomegranates. The idea is that Christ has come to conquer death decisively, not for six months here and six months there, so that we can say, with Saint Paul, "O grave, where is thy victory? O death, where is thy sting?" It is also fitting that the juice of the pomegranate is a deep blood red, like the rich blood that Jesus will shed for us, and that will become for us our spiritual drink.

The *pomegranate* is a Latin compound, a *pomum granatum,* a *grainapple,* we might say. It has about the shape and size of an apple, but is full of soft seeds, each covered with a wrap of sweet and juicy pulp, about the size of a kernel of corn. The thing is, the *pomegranate* isn't a *pome* at all. A pome is a fruit like an apple, with an edible skin and flesh, around a core that contains inedible seeds. A pear is a pome. A quince is a pome. A pomegranate isn't.

What do we call those fruits that are filled with edible seeds scattered all about, and edible pulp, with a rind or a skin that we sometimes eat and sometimes don't? We call them *berries.* The pomegranate is a berry, like the blueberry and the strawberry—and the orange and the tomato! Don't be fooled by the size; the tomato is a berry. The Italians, looking again at the size and shape and color, and not what's inside, call the tomato a *pomo-doro,* a *goldenapple;* a word that sure is finer than *tomato.* The French don't call them that, but they do have a nice word for another edible staple that isn't a pome: *pomme de terre, groundapple,* the humble *potato.* You say *potato,* I say *tomato,* but ain't neither one of them a pome.

Nor is something else suggested by the shape of the thing, from the French word for *pomegranate: grenade.*

Fair is foul, foul is fair,
Hover through the fog and filthy air!

So cry out the three Weird Sisters in the first scene of
Macbeth. Their equivocation is going to be echoed in
a moment by the blood-drenched and victorious Macbeth, who says to his companion Banquo, "So foul and
fair a day I have not seen." Dear Macbeth of the ambiguous morals, you haven't seen anything yet.

The word *foul* in American English now enjoys its
most common use in sports. If a lineman takes a cheap
shot at the quarterback after he's thrown the football,
the referee will call him for a *personal foul,* roughing the
passer, fifteen yards and an automatic first down. If
the defender on the basketball court leaps up and
catches the hand of his opponent while he's making a
shot, that's a *foul,* and if he racks up five of them, he's
out of the game. The batter in baseball who hits the ball
outside of the chalk lines has hit a *foul*—if it weren't for
the foul rule, we'd have to play baseball in the round,
like cricket. In the very early days of baseball, a foul
ball wasn't a strike, but then somebody, and may he
be forever blessed, came up with the beautiful idea of
calling it a strike for the first two but not for the third;
a perfect compromise. The odd thing, though, about
baseball is that a ball that strikes the *foul line* is not
foul but *fair,* and a ball that strikes the *foul pole* is fair

and a home run. The rule makes perfect sense, but the usage doesn't; why don't we call them the *fair lines* and the *fair pole?*

The old meaning of *foul*, though, has nothing to do with sports or judgments, but with disgust. Something *foul* has a stench about it: a *foul smell.* That made it easy to apply the word to heinous actions: *foul play.* It's rotten, it stinks. That is one of the leading themes of *Hamlet*, too. Everybody recalls the reaction of the soldier, when the Ghost of the old King Hamlet appears: "Something is rotten in the state of Denmark." That Ghost, when he finally has the chance to speak with Hamlet Junior, says that his time is short, because he must at daybreak return to purgatory (he may be lying about that; he may be from hell, we don't know), where he must abide *"till the foul crimes done in my days of nature / Are burnt and purged away."* However foul those crimes were, they couldn't possibly be as bad as pouring poison into your brother's ear while he's sleeping, and then marrying his widow ten minutes later. The memory of that crime drives the new king Claudius to his knees:

> *O my offense is rank, it smells to Heaven;*
> *It hath the primal eldest curse upon it,*
> *A brother's murder.*

The noun for *foul* is one of those old sorts in English, made up of a verb or an adjective, followed by the ancient suffix *-ith.* The *i* in the suffix caused *umlaut,* or vowel-change, in the previous suffix, moving it by anticipation to the front of the mouth, where *-ith* is going to be pronounced. That's why we have *broad,*

breadth; long, length; strong, strength; and *foul, filth.*
That's the noun right there. It now suggests soiling of
a particularly wet and nasty or smelly sort; a kid who
has just been building sandcastles is not *filthy,* but the
kid who has been fishing for frogs in the swamp is.
The filth may be moral, too: porn is *filth,* and the people
who produce it are *foul.*

intellect

What is the one thing that politicians of our day lack the
most? Honesty? Courage? Piety? Humility?

I often hear the phrase "freedom of choice," which is
supposed to denote the greatest freedom that an American or any human being can enjoy. That's absurd. You
go to a delicatessen, with these plates on offer: Rotten
Eggs; Cardboard; Stinging Nettle; Black Bananas with
Axle Grease; Mystery Slop; Sugared Sawdust and Glue;
Unwashed Pig Intestine; and Spam.

"But I don't *like* Spam!" you say.

"Well, what of it? Look at all the other dishes. You
have *freedom of choice!*"

"I'll have the Spam."

The point is that human freedom and flourishing depend not upon our having choices, but upon
our having the inner freedom—a liberating virtue,
hard-won—to make *right choices.* The wrong choices
enslave. It may look like liberty to choose among one of
the dishes above, but it's a liberty to choose which stuff

is going to make your gorge rise up. It may look like liberty to have your choice among fifty ways to descend lower than a beast, but that's a liberty to choose the color of your manacles and fetters. They may come in all the colors of the rainbow, but they are still going to chain you to the post.

And this is where *intellect* comes in. Not will, mind you, or wantonness, but the *intellect,* which is that power whereby we see what is right and "choose" it in the mind, directing our will to comply. The word comes from the medieval schoolmen: *intellectus,* which denotes vision, an immediate insight into truth—the distinctive way whereby angels know, also given in part to man. The noun is built from the perfect participle of the verb *intelligere* = *inter* + *legere, to choose among.* In Latin, to read is *legere, to pick out the words* of a text; not the easiest thing in the world to do, back before the convention of spaces between words, and lower case letters. That is why people back then read out loud only. The voice helped you figure out when a word began and when it ended.

Something of the moral value of the right and intelligent choice remains in our words that have to do with choosing. An *elite* school (from the French, ultimately from Latin *eligere, to pick out;* English *elect*) is truly *select* (from Latin *selectus, chosen and set aside*) and *choice* (used as an adjective, to describe good cuts of beef, rare coins, and waterfront property). But that's still quite a descent from the highest purpose of the intellect, which is to behold with wonder what is true and good and beautiful: to see the face of God. Hence the beginning of Dante's *Paradiso:*

The glory of the One who moves all things
penetrates the universe with light,
more radiant in one part and elsewhere less;
I have been in that heaven He makes most
bright,
and seen things neither mind can hold nor
tongue
utter, when one descends from that great
height,
For as we near the One for whom we long,
our intellects so plunge into the deep,
memory cannot follow where we go.
Nevertheless what small part I can keep
of that holy kingdom treasured in my heart
will now become the matter of my song.

When Virgil and Dante are on the shores of the Mountain of Purgatory, they meet a venerable old man who asks them what they are doing there, since it's evident that they have not arrived by the usual means. Virgil, who recognizes the man but who does not name him for us, replies that he is not one of the souls damned to eternal punishment for sins committed, that Dante is still alive, and that they have embarked upon this strange journey at the permission and direction of a lady from above. And the reason for the journey? *Libertà va cercando,* Virgil says of his charge:

He seeks his liberty: and how dear that is,
he who refused his life for it knows well.
You know it, for you did not think it bitter
to die for liberty in Utica,
where you sloughed off the garment that shall
*   shine*
So bright on the great day.

The old man is Cato the Younger, called Cato of Utica, who, when he saw that his armies massed in that city in northern Africa would not suffice to put down the ambitions of Pompey and Caesar, took his own life. Not in despair, as Dante reads it, but, taking his cue from the poet Lucan, as a testimony to the inestimable value of freedom. In Lucan's poem, Cato says that he wishes he could give himself, one for all mankind, to die so that they would all be free.

It's doubtful that Lucan was thinking only of political liberty, an absence of restraint, extrinsic to the human soul. No great poet or philosopher or theologian thought of it that way, and Dante certainly didn't either. Dante will ascend the Mountain of Purgatory not to attain some voting rights or other, but to attain the only true freedom which is intrinsic to the soul, a freedom from the manacles and fetters of sin. Imagine what joy would be ours, if for even a day we could be entirely free of the tugs and pinches—or the straitjackets!—of pride, envy, wrath, acedia, avarice, gluttony, and lust. Yes, our economy would collapse; but then we might be able to build something genuinely human upon its ruins.

The word *free* has a rich history, which suggests many associations with the fullness of human flourishing, and not just political machinery or a negative against the will of others who would impose theirs upon us. That last, by the way, is Satan's definition in *Paradise Lost*, when he sees the miserable stretches of Infernal Detroit and, as always refusing to see that true liberty is indivisible from virtue, including obedience, says, *Here at least we shall be free.* If that is all that freedom is, a negative, a lack of restraint, then to hell with it. That is a freedom for somebody eager to suffer the worst form of enslavement: to himself and his sinful passions. But the Old English *freo* suggests something precious, to rejoice in, to hold dear: it is related to the German words *Friede, peace,* and *Freude, joy*—and *Frau, wife!*

In English the word also suggests a generous and openhearted approach to the world. "Freely have you received," says Jesus; "freely give" (Mt 10:8). To be *free* in this sense is to be hearty and healthy, affirming the goodness of the world, and not ashamed to be entirely open to that goodness. When the blind Gloucester in *King Lear* teeters on the brink of despair, his son Edgar, playing the role of spiritual physician, counsels him to *bear free and patient thoughts.* Words in the Romance languages that convey the same meaning, though etymologically unrelated to *free,* have enriched our English too, giving us *gratis, gratitude,* and, most important of all, *grace.*

Speed

Sometimes, when somebody is about to embark on a trip around the world in a hot air balloon, you'll hear a well-wisher from the crowd cry out, *"God-speed!"* By this epithet I gather he means, "May God give you a quick journey!" Not too quick, though, unless the traveler wishes to land only a few hundred miles away and in Iowa, and then think how sorry he would be.

The funny thing about that use of the word is that *godspeed* does not have anything to do with God, and only tangentially anything to do with *speed.* The first syllable is the Old English adjective *god,* pronounced *goad,* meaning *good:* so when the monks came to evangelize the pagan Saxons, they translated the Greco-Latin *evangelium* = *eu* + *angelion* = *good tid-ings* into Anglo-Saxon *god* + *spel* = *good report, good account.* Hence the English *gospel,* unusual in Euro-pean languages—quite different from Italian *vangelio,* German *Evangel,* Welsh *efengyl.*

The *speed* part of the word, too, doesn't principally have to do with velocity. It means *success,* as in the name of the flower: *speedwell.* So, then, *godspeed* means *good success,* or *good luck:* cf. French *bonne chance,* Italian *auguri.* When Saint Peter, in Milton's *Lycidas,* inveighs against the ravenous preachers of heresy, wolves in sheep's clothing, he says that the hungry sheep look up, but what do the wolves care? *They are sped,* meaning *they enjoy the success they have sought* or, as Jesus puts it sardonically, *they have their reward.* And yet, if you are going on a journey, *speed* might well be a good part of its success—so the word in Anglo-Saxon which *did not* really refer to velocity, but which *now* does, once did, long *before* Anglo-Saxon days in England. Apparently *speed* sped around the semantic track and succeeded in recover-ing its original sense.

Related to anything in Latin? Yes: *spes, hope.* That Latin word carries the sense of looking forward; so that somebody who hopes for good speed in the future is engaging in the action denoted by the Latin verb *prosperare,* in which the s has changed into *r* by the process known as rhotacization, which is the process by which a letter changes into *r.* (This jest will be another entry in my forthcoming volume "The Lonely Lives of Philologists.") Shakespeare therefore gave that name to the now foolishly maligned hero of *The Tempest: Prospero, I look forward with hope.* The word also provides us with one of the titles of Mary: *Mater Spei, Mother of Hope.* From the French *desespoir,* a *dis-sperare,* we derive English *despair,* the ultimate sin and perhaps the worst punishment for sin. "Despair and die," say the spirits of all whom Shakespeare's Richard III has murdered, appearing to him one after another in a dream on the night before his fatal battle at Bosworth Field. "Be valiant, and speed well!" says Lord Stanley to Richard's opponent the Earl of Richmond, on that same night. He will.

Athanasius

Athanasius contra mundum, Athanasius against the world—that was Saint Athanasius, the irrepressible and fearless bishop of Alexandria, fighting against the Arian heresy, which reduced Christ to a being preeminent among creatures, and not one in being with the Father.

If that seems abstruse and of no importance to the daily life of the Christian, we have Chesterton to remind us that the verse "God is Love" makes no sense whatsoever unless God Himself is a communion of love, prior to and outside of anything He might create. The verse sounds sentimental but is a theological thunderclap, tearing open the veil to give man a glimpse of the inner life of the Godhead. The Athanasian Creed sounds abstract and polemical, but is warm with life and truth.

I have a warm spot in my heart for two more famouses Athanasiuses. One was a Jesuit priest, a contemporary of Galileo, a scientist and polymath named Athanasius Kircher. Father Kircher was apparently quite a character. One time he had himself lowered into the crater of Mount Vesuvius, which had erupted a few years before. He wanted to check things out for himself, back in the days before cameras. There's another Athanasius whom baseball fans in Cincinnati may remember. He was Hispanic, and his baptismal name was *Atanasio Perez, Athanasius Perez.* His family called him by the diminutive *Tany,* which English speakers heard all wrong, calling him by my name, *Tony.* Yes, the cheerful hard-fighting slugger for the Big Red Machine, Tony Perez, was named *Athanasius* after the cheerful hard-fighting slugger of a saint.

The name is Greek, and is made up of two elements. The first is the alpha-privative prefix *a-,* meaning *without, free from, not characterized by.* Modern English speakers have adopted the prefix, so it is quite "live" for us: a farmer may be *moral,* while a politician is *amoral;* when the senator speaks rubbish, that is *typical,* but if he stumbles into sense, that is *atypical.* The second element is built from the Greek *thanatos, death:* someone who is *Athanasius* is *death-less;* or, translating into Latin, *im-mortal.* Grimm tells us that Greek *th* = Germanic *d,* and Greek *t* = Germanic *th,* so it is possible, not certain, that Greek *thanatos* is lying in the same morgue with English *death.*

But most words in the Indo-European languages take their words for dying from a different root, the one that gives us Latin **morts > mors, death* (cf. Welsh *marw, to die*). Even we in English did so, not for dying but for making somebody else die, in a nasty and underhanded way: Old English *morthor,* murder. We don't usually lose our *th's,* going from Old English to Modern English, and for quite a while we had a fight to the death between *murther,* the native word, and *murder,* from Anglo-Norman—those Frenchies never liked the *th.* In Shakespeare we find *murther,* actually quite a lot of it, though how Shakespeare wrote the word and spoke it, and what the editor or publisher did on his own, we can't really tell. Anyway, here is the Thoroughly Modern Millie Macbeth:

> *Come to my woman's breasts*
> *And take my milk for gall, you murthering*
> *   ministers,*
> *Wherever in your sightless substances*
> *You wait for nature's mischief!*

Eventually *murder* won out, but not *farder* and *furder.*

music

Our play's *The Merchant of Venice.* The newlyweds
Lorenzo and Jessica are out on the portico at night, await-
ing the return of Portia, the mistress of the house, while
music to welcome her is played within. The lovely couple
have just engaged in a sweet and merry teasing competition, musical in itself, and now, in the calm, Jessica says,
"I am never merry when I hear sweet music." She doesn't
mean, as modern directors who don't know English,
Shakespeare, dramaturgy, or music seem to think, that
she is not happy. Quite the contrary. She means that her
merriment has given way to a deep solemnity, akin to joy.

"The reason is," Lorenzo replies, "your spirits are
attentive." And then Lorenzo gives us an eloquent
description of the power of music, the "touches of
sweet harmony" that can cause the beasts themselves
to change their nature, to still the heat of their blood.
"The man that hath no music in himself," he says,

> *Nor is not moved with concord of sweet sounds,*
> *Is fit for treasons, stratagems, and spoils;*
> *The motions of his spirit are dull as night,*
> *And his affections dark as Erebus.*
> *Let no such man be trusted. Mark the music.*

I leave to the reader to draw inferences about how
Shakespeare is taught by all-day, all-political critics,

and about our mass phenomena generally, heavy as it is with political chatter, gabble, snarling, and bellowing, and short, so short, on music. And what music we do profess to have goes out of its way to be inane and ugly. My dog Jasper is wiser: when I play (poorly, but I try) Bach chorales on the piano, he lies at my feet, and sometimes climbs into the chair. Last night he lay on my lap and rested his chin on my wrist, which made me have to improvise a bit to keep him comfortable.

The word *music* comes straight from Latin *musica,* borrowed from Greek *mousike,* the art of the *Muses,* daughters of Zeus and Mnemosyne, the goddess of memory. The nine Muses inspire men with knowledge of the arts, which in those days included such things as astronomy and history. The stars, playing music? Yes, certainly, since the Greeks sensed that all the world was an expression of order and harmony. You can't get far in ancient, medieval, or Renaissance literature without a sense for that love of harmony; hence Sir John Davies' most famous poem, *Orchestra,* is a long witty come-on by Antinous, chief of the suitors at the home of the long-gone Odysseus. He is trying to persuade Penelope to dance with him. For the universe itself is a great harmony, even if we think of the tiny particles of matter that make it up:

> *They err that say they did concur by chance:*
> *Love made them meet in a well-ordered dance.*

Just about all of the poets and artists and even the theologians and philosophers from Pythagoras to Milton would have agreed.

In 1872, Captain Charles Boycott, himself a farmer
also, became the Land Agent for a group of English
landowners in Ireland. The nineteenth century wasn't
very kind to Irish agriculture, probably because
of the Little Ice Age, from which we've recovered,
thank the Lord. When Captain Boycott's tenants came
to ask him to lower their rents, he not only told them
that he was not authorized to do that. He started to
evict them. The Irish Land League responded by orga-
nizing all the servants and hired hands and retail-
ers and purchasers in the neighborhood, to unite
against him by refusing to have anything more to do
with him. Boycott couldn't do a damned thing about it,
and finally he and his family had to return to England.
That form of labor-driven ostracism caught on, and
became known by the name of the man against whom
it was first directed: the *boycott*. Riccardo Bacchelli,
a severely underrated Italian novelist of the twentieth
century, records in *The Mill on the Po* that that word
which sounded very strange to the Italian ear entered
their language very soon after the events in Ireland,
as tenant workers and small merchants near Ferrr-
ara united in a *boycott* against their "enemy," a man
who was several decades ahead of them in agricultural
techniques, and whose farms were prospering. They
being Italians, it didn't quite work, but it did help to

bring about political confusion, which is often better than political efficiency, because it means that politicians who mean mischief don't get much done.

So we have here a word that comes from somebody's name, and the name is all but forgotten. That happens sometimes. One of the most brilliant men of the Middle Ages, Blessed John of Scotland, is excruciatingly difficult to read. So English writers in the Renaissance sniffed at him and his kind, because they hadn't the patience to master the philosophy. John of Scotland is better known by his half-Latinized half-Scots name, Duns Scotus, and from that name we get our word *dunce*. That says a good deal more about post-Renaissance prejudices than it says about the Subtle Doctor. A favorite anecdote of mine: a woman once brought her young son to the ornery Thomas Carlyle, to see if she could enlist that odd and remarkable mind to instruct the lad, because school hadn't worked out for him. Said Carlyle, in a broad northern accent, "Air ye sure he's no' a doonce?"

Captain Boycott deserved it, and Duns Scotus didn't. But sometimes it works out well, and your name becomes a word for something which, if it isn't quite wonderful, is at least respectable. If you're in Italy and you're at Saint Peter's or in the Piazza della Signoria in Florence or at Saint Mark's in Venice or any of the five thousand astounding places in that country, take good note of the Italian tour guide—I almost wrote the "handsome Italian" tour guide, but that would be redundant, wouldn't it? That eloquent speaker to the crowds is *un cicerone: a Cicero.*

barbarian

This word goes all the way back to Indo-European times, to describe somebody who *babbles* (that's how we put it in English), or who has just come down from the Tower of *Babel* and can't say anything that anybody can understand (that's how they put it in Hebrew). It's an imitative word, to echo somebody stammering or blubbering or spluttering—that is, speaking gibberish, nonsense. "No more blah blah!" cries Captain Kirk to the gang of kids threatening to bonk bonk him on the head because he's a Grup. And who says that great art is dead?

But this particular word comes to us from the Greek *barbaros,* and in democratic Athens it didn't just mean somebody whose language sounded like *bar-bar-bar.* It meant somebody who did not enjoy the advantage of being Greek. That had little to do with ethnicity, and a lot to do with culture and politics—the affairs of the *polis.* Essentially, if you lived in a place where you had no real say in affairs that should most concern a free man—let's say, in what your schools should be teaching and how, or in which businesses might set up shop in your town, or what kinds of festivals your town may celebrate, or what kinds of addresses might be spoken at such festivals—then you are a *barbarian.* It isn't your fault, or at least not much your fault.

My favorite example of barbarians is found in Aristophanes' play, *The Acharnians.* Athens and Sparta have recently declared war on one another, and Aristophanes is incensed over its folly and over what he believes are corrupt politicians benefiting personally and "professionally" from the war, at the expense of the people. So we are treated in the opening of the play to a "democratic" assembly in Athens, clearly rigged, while self-interested Athenian politicians bring out an absurdly tall ambassador from Persia to speak to the assembly. The Persian ambassador is there to persuade them to ally themselves with Persia against the Spartans. That alone is meant to be infuriating to a patriotic Athenian audience. Why on earth should any Greek submit himself to that rich and ambitious empire of barbarians, just to win help in a war against fellow Greeks? To show the treachery of it all, Aristophanes has the ambassador speak in a Persian-sounding gibberish, which has to be "translated" to the assembly by Athenian politicians in the Persian pay. Even at that, the Persian "promises" are couched in ambiguous terms that barely hide their malignity and contempt for the Greeks. "See!" cry the politicians. "We're going to get all that gold they promise!" A base motive, even if the Persians could be trusted.

But I still haven't described the most important feature of this barbarian. He has only one eye, a big one right in the middle of his forehead. In other words, the Persian is a cyclops—the idiot from the *Odyssey,* one of those big sheep-herding lugs who don't give a damn about the common good, on that rich and untended island where every family ignores its neighbors. Now, the Persian barbarians don't have an untended island. They have a vast empire and efficient armies, bureaucrats, and couriers—Herodotus' praise of those couriers has become the unofficial motto of our Snail Mail Service. You know, neither rain nor snow nor sleet nor lunch hours nor crazy office workers brandishing pistols keep them from their appointed rounds. So these barbarians have a government, and more's the pity, because nobody has any real say in it. They suffer the edicts of imperial officers from afar, from Ecbatana on the Potomac.

One more thing about the ambassador: he is called the Great Eye of the Emperor. That's one of the functions of the imperial officers, to see everything and report on it. A well-oiled surveillance state: *barbara, et apta semiviris et servis.* I hope I don't need to translate that. I will anyway: "Barbarous, and fit for half-men and slaves."

If you ever go to the Arena Chapel in Padua, be sure to check out the background of Giotto's series of panels depicting events from the life of Jesus. You'll see a persistent rocky hill with a flourishing tree atop it. But when you get to the panel depicting the deposition of Christ from the cross, that same tree on the hill will be denuded of all leaves.

Early on in Christian hymnody, we find subtle meditations upon the Cross as a tree. From Venantius Fortunatus' hymn, chanted during Holy Week in the Roman Missal:

Blest Tree, whose happy branches bore
the wealth that did the world restore;
the beam that did that Body weigh
which raised up Hell's expected prey.

From Claudianus Mamertus' hymn, also chanted during Holy Week:

Eating of the Tree forbidden,
Man had sunk in Satan's snare,
When his pitying Creator
Did this second Tree prepare;
Destined, many ages later,
That first evil to repair.

The tree of the Cross is foreshadowed by the Tree of Life, in Genesis—or is in plain fact the same Tree of Life. So John Donne suggests:

We think that Paradise and Calvary,
Christ's cross and Adam's tree, stood in one place;
Look, Lord, and find both Adams met in me;
As the first Adam's sweat surrounds my face,
May the last Adam's blood my soul embrace.
                    —*Hymn to God, My God, In My Sickness,*
                                        John Donne

But perhaps the most beautiful depiction of the Cross as the Tree of Life is to be found in the magnificent green and gold mosaic of Saint Clement's in Rome—a luxuriant tree of many branches and leaves, nourished by the blood of Christ, and curling its tendrils out towards all the universe.

May all of your sins and sorrows be nailed to the Cross.

The evening before Easter Sunday, Christians celebrate the Easter Vigil, and all over the world people will be baptized and confirmed in the evening service, and given their first taste of the bread of heaven, having all sweetness within it.

The word *vigil* suggests being awake, especially during those hours when most people are asleep. So we say that someone *keeps vigil* at the bedside of a dying friend, waiting through the night, ready to minister any small comforts he can, praying, and giving small but sure tokens of love. In fact, Latin *vigilare* is cognate with English *wake* and *watch*, and those English words are twins. It's what happened when the same word split along two phonetic tracks, and each one survived, assuming slightly different meanings: cf. *screech, shriek; tow, tug; bow, bay; an, one.* The sense of *vigilance* in English *watch* is preserved in a variety of phrases: *night watchman, watch out, on the watch.* It is wonderfully expressed in the opening lines of the English translation of the mighty hymn *Vigiles et sancti:*

Ye watchers and ye holy ones,
Bright Seraphs, Cherubim, and Thrones,
Raise the glad strain, Alleluia!
Cry out, Dominions, Princedoms, Powers,
Virtues, Archangels, Angel choirs,
Alleluia, alleluia, alleluia, alleluia, alleluia!

That does not mean that the Seraphs are waiting for a surprise. It means that they are alert, alive, immersed in the vision of God.

On the evening before the battle of Bosworth Field, Shakespeare's tyrant Richard III is fretful, sluggish of spirit, acutely aware of the passing hours; and when he sleeps, he dreams, and the dreams bring him no comfort: there come to him the spirits of all the people he has murdered. "Tomorrow in the battle think on me," says his brother Clarence, "And fall thy edgeless sword. Despair and die." Meanwhile, his rival Richmond readies himself for the morrow by encouraging his men and saying a short evening prayer, echoing the words of compline:

> *O Thou whose captain I account myself,*
> *Look on my forces with a gracious eye.*
> *Put in their hands thy bruising irons of wrath,*
> *That they may crush down with a heavy fall*
> *The usurping helmets of our adversaries!*
> *Make us thy ministers of chastisement,*
> *That we may praise Thee in the victory!*
> *To Thee I do commend my watchful soul,*
> *Ere I let fall the windows of mine eyes.*
> *Sleeping and waking, O defend me still.*

My freshmen, by the way, could make no sense of the word *watchful* in those lines; they were not aware that it had to do with *waking*. Nor did they catch the allusion in the last lines: "Father, into your hands I commend my spirit."

Come the next Holy Saturday, remember that we watch, that night, by the tomb of Christ.

Slack

Have you ever noticed that there aren't any words in French or Spanish that begin with *sl-*? There weren't any in Latin either. Every language rules out certain combinations of consonants, as being too hard to pronounce. Hawaiian rules them all out! You never get two consonants together in Hawaiian, but you sure get a lot of vowels to make up for them.

Now then, we know that the English language is a cousin of French and Spanish—and Latin. Either Latin lost *all the words* that survive in English beginning with *sl-* (and in German, beginning with *schl-*), or the words are there, but they're hidden. It's the latter. Latin speakers didn't like the *sl*, just as in Middle English we stopped liking *kn-* and *wr-*, ending up pronouncing only *n* and *r*. The Latins dropped the *s*; or we may say that it was assimilated or absorbed into the following *l,* for ease of pronunciation. It's why we say *collect* instead of *conlect* and *aggressive* instead of *adgressive*.

The root idea underlying the *sl-* words is that of fluidity or softness or weakness: *slow, slug, slink, slick.* The Latin relatives of our *sl-* words begin with *l-*. So *slack* is related to Latin *languere,* to *languish,* to lie about, to be *lax* (from the past participle, *laxus*). So a *slacker* is *lax,* by definition! When we *relax* discipline, we run the risk of raising a generation of people who are *loose,* who have no moral sinews. Then things grow really *slippery:* an *sl* cousin of *lubricate* and *lubricious.* We *slip* into immorality: an *sl* cousin of *lapse.*

Another odd thing about the *sl-* opening is that it seems to be still active—that is, productive of new words. We didn't use to slosh around in slush, in English. When C. S. Lewis named the devil in charge of "education" Slubgob, he surely had in mind all the slack slumping sluggish slimy words that had long been slinking about in the linguistic slums. But everybody's favorite slug coinage has to be that of another Lewis, Carroll:

> *'Twas brillig, and the slithy toves*
> *Did gyre and gimble in the wabe;*
> *All mimsy were the borogoves,*
> *And the mome raths outgrabe.*

I wish I'd said that!

The study of words, as Lewis and Tolkien knew, is a study of man. And that is why modern literary theorists shy away from immersing themselves in languages and from close and sensitive attention to the meanings of words. Words, because they harbor anthropological truth, are understandable across cultures and run athwart political programs, which come

and go. But when the garden of words is not tended,
weeds grow thick and rank. Orwell tried to tell us
about that.

Our word today, *wrong*, is an anthropological case
in point. It has relations all over the Indo-European
languages. Its initial consonant pair, *wr*, which was
pronounced as such, gives us plenty of words in
the Germanic languages that have to do with twisting or turning: English *wrist, wrench, wry, writhe,
wring, worry, wire*, and many more; German *werfen, to throw*; *wuergeln, to strangle* (cf. Latin *ver-
tere, to turn*). *Wrong* is one of those words. The sense
is that if something isn't straight, "direct," *right*, it
is *wrong*, twisted, bent, deformed. A *queer* feeling in
your belly suggests that you are sick or that the rus-
tling noise around the corner is not the wind. Someone with a *warped* mind is deranged in a peculiarly
sinister way.

We see the same point illustrated also by unrelated words in other languages. Latin *pravus* suggests
something crooked, especially in a moral sense: hence
depraved. "*Guai a voi, anime prave*," cries Charon to
the wretched souls gathered at the shores of the Acheron. "*Woe to you, crooked souls*," as one translator
I know has put it. "I am not a *crook*," said President
Nixon. We don't like to engage a businessman whose
actions depart from the straight way of plain dealing: he
is *devious*. We are rightly suspicious of someone who
speaks in *circumlocutions*, words that take us round
and round without getting straight to the point.

Many other words that have to do with evil suggest
a stench, as English *foul*, Italian *puttana*, *whore* (a

female stinker), as opposed to what is pure: English *clean*, German *rein*, Welsh *glan*, Greek *katharos*. There's nothing *fishy* about such words.

feminine

Words for men and women are anthropological gold, because they present across cultures and millennia the basic human insights into the two sexes. Some are descriptive, some are honorific, and some fall into pejoratives; and this is true of words for either sex. English *man* and *woman* are markers for the categories and nothing more. Italian *uomo* is both the general word for *human being* and the specific word for adult male; but the Italian word for woman is the old honorific *donna*, from Latin *domina*, the lady, the female head of the household. That is a higher honor even than Swedish *kvinna*, which is related to English *queen*, but simply means *woman*, while Italian suggests a certain admiration: hence *Madonna*, *my Lady*, to refer affectionately and reverently to Mary.

Sometimes the word for *man* suggests toughness and bravery. That is behind Greek *aner*, whose genitive, *andros*, gives us the name *Andrew*, and such coinages as *androgen*, *androsterone*, and so forth (cf. the distant Welsh cousin *nerth*, *power*). More often it's just the generic for human being, applied specifically to men. The old folk etymology connecting *human* with *humus*, *soil*, may well be valid; the same idea is present in Hebrew *Adam / Adamah*.

Words for women often suggest something special that women do, or some distinguishing feature of their bodies. In Italian, your husband is your *marito*, the man you are married to, but your wife is not your "*marita*." Your wife is your *moglie* (cf. Spanish *mujer*), pronounced *moh-lyeh*, from Latin *mulier*. That word is related to Latin *mollis*, *soft* (cf. English *mollify*), usually with a pleasant sense. Someone who is softhearted may *melt* with pity. It is a wicked thing to be hard of heart, and a foolish thing to be soft in the head; it is sometimes but not always a virtue to be hardheaded, and sometimes but not always a virtue to be softhearted. It is a virtue to be *manly*, but a vice to be *mannish*; a virtue to be *womanly*, but a vice to be *womanish*. The sense is that we ought to be grateful when the properties natural to each sex grow up healthy and strong, and that we ought to be wary when a member of one sex attempts to mimic the habits, more likely the vices than the virtues, of the other sex. For vices are easy to mimic, as caricaturists well know. Virtues are not.

temperance

Wherever the Catholic sun doth shine
There's always laughter and good red wine.
At least I've always found it so:
Benedicamus Domino!

So wrote the redoubtable Hilaire Belloc in *The Path to Rome,* the book in which he shows his holiday humor to best effect. That bulldog of a man decided to tramp from Rheims to Rome over the course of two weeks, climbing mountains, fording rivers, getting stuck in swamps, swearing in mock-Italian at a couple of *carabinieri*, scrounging up food and drink and making it to the Eternal City in time for the feast of Corpus Christi.

I'll forgive Belloc for forgetting that Lutheran Germans liked their wine too, and their beer. By the time he was vagabonding to Rome, "temperance" movements in the English speaking countries had long been waging war against alcoholic drinks. The war would culminate in the Volstead Act, that great progressive-era amendment that tried to wring America dry. It worked, sort of. It did deliver a body blow to alcoholic consumption in the United States, and actuarial tables for the years following show a steep decline, then a leveling, in deaths related to cirrhosis of the liver. But it also spawned organized crime, and a huge federal agency to fight the organized crime, and when the Volstead Act was repealed, the G-men were not.

There were temperance societies everywhere, too, not just in the United States, and not just among Protestants: The Knights of Father Mathew boasted a large troop of Irish coal miners in the small town where I grew up, strong men, nothing of the sissy about them, who "took the pledge." It is strange, though, that temperance, one of the four cardinal virtues, should have been reduced to such a narrow range: tee-totaling. I don't suppose we will soon see a temperance society for Watching Less Television, or a temperance society for the Relief of Overscheduled Children, or a temperance society to put Jabba the State on a saccharine and water diet. "I eat Metrecal with a fork," said a slender blonde in a commercial from my boyhood, as she sipped the low-cal liquid from the tines. I wish I could put Uncle Sam on Metrecal and make him eat it with a fork too.

It's too bad that the word has come to be associated only with drink. Its range in classical and Christian philosophy is vast. Temperance has to do with the body, yes, but also with the passions and the intellect. It is the virtue of the judicious measure. It usually but not always implies that we must hold some desire in check, or direct it aright, as a horseman directs the horse. Occasionally it means that we must give some flagging desire a kick to get it going. It is opposed to touchiness and to insensibility, to cowardice and to recklessness, to dullness and to a vicious curiosity, to sluggishness and to frenzy: to losing your *temper*.

The old meaning of the word shines out in Bach's "Well Tempered Clavier," the Clavier whose notes are compromised ingeniously so that Bach could play a melody in any key, and it would not turn into wave-mud. Something *tempered* obeys direction. It is like a rudder in good working order. Someone who is *temperate* is skilled with that rudder. It obeys his touch, as he pays heed to the wind and the weather. Book Two of Edmund Spenser's *The Faerie Queene* is devoted to Sir Guyon, the Knight of Temperance, and therefore much of the book has to do with the hierarchical obedience that characterizes a healthy body or a healthy body politic. Sure enough, the book's climax does feature a boat with a rudder, a passenger, an oarsman, and a captain. The relationship between *temperance* and *government* becomes quite clear when we remember that, literally, the Greek *kybernetes* (Latin *gubernator*) is the helmsman, the man who holds the rudder. Despotism and the rule of the rabble—*democracy*—are both examples of *intemperance*, in Spenser's scheme. That suspicion of democracy, and the sense that it is the fraternal twin of despotism, goes all the way back to Plato. Many of our Founding Fathers, who read their Spenser and their Plato, agreed.

One of the prime candidates for most notoriously altered word must be Machiavelli's use of the Italian *vertù* in his handbook for amoral and effective politicians, *The Prince*. The word hovers between what we would now call *virtuosity*, as applied to playing not a violin but one's enemies, rivals, courtiers, and subjects, and *virility*, manliness, or rather machismo. For Fortune is a woman, says Old Nick, and favors young men because they are impetuous and masterful and go at it with no nonsense.

There's also a neutral and abstract sense of the word that prevails in Middle English and survives in one or two fossilized phrases in Modern English. Herbs, potions, and stones were thought to possess (and sometimes did possess) *virtues*, that is, *powers* for acting upon the body. So the VIRTUE of the herb eyebright was to help clear your vision, and the *virtue* of feverfew was to cool you down. In movies we hear a justice of the peace, marrying a young couple, say, "By *virtue* of the power vested in me, I now pronounce you man and wife," meaning that he can do so because of a potency he possesses by his office.

The word itself comes from Latin *virtus*, which had a range of meanings even in the classical authors: so temperance, courage, wisdom, and prudence are *virtutes*, *virtues*, as we would call them too. Its inner meaning is what Machiavelli played upon: the quality of being a real *vir*, *a man*. Manliness, then, is what the Romans first thought of when they used the word. They didn't simply mean that one was an adult male. Any boy will grow up to be an adult male, but growing up to be a *vir* is different. So the Romans encouraged the boy to live up to that difference, robing him with the *toga virilis*, the *manly toga*, when he was twelve years old. It was the Roman version of the Hebrew bar mitzvah (literally, "son of the commandment") and the gruesome and excruciating Sun Dance of the Plains Indians: a rite of passage for the boy, marking a fundamental change.

An adverbial form of the word shows up in Jerome's translation of Saint Paul's words to the men of Corinth: *viriliter agite*, a rendering of the Greek *andrizeisthe*, and happily translated in English as *quit ye like men*; Shakespeare may well be echoing those words when he has King Alonso cry out to the mariners in *The Tempest*, "Play the men!"—for Saint Paul and ships in danger of wreck were on our playwright's mind. "Not a hair perished," says Ariel, reporting to Prospero, and alluding to Paul's promise to the terrified mariners in Acts. Contemporary translations expunge the allusion to manhood, so clear in both the Latin and the Greek, and advise us merely to *be courageous*, as if we actually were suffering from an excess of manliness out there.

The most revolutionary words ever uttered were not spoken by man. They were spoken by God. Recall the scene. Moses has been living in exile from his native Egypt, tending sheep in the Sinai for his father-in-law, Jethro. All at once he sees something that seems impossible. A bush is burning, but it is not consumed. We might notice right here that if Moses were making something up to justify his claim to have been sent by God, he would think of something more impressive than a bush on fire. There is something quiet, small, uncanny about it. Moses approaches, and then begins the great conversation.

"When the children of Israel ask me, what shall I say is your name?"

Let us pause to observe that the pagan gods, like human beings, and their horses and their dogs, have names. The name draws a kind of sacred circle around a thing, and to give a name to someone is to exercise authority over him. Here is the critical moment. Will we have a god—a Mr. Apollo, a big creature within the universe, to be identified with some feature of that universe, like thunder (Thor), or corn (Ceres), or the ocean (Poseidon), or the sun (Amon-Ra), or the Roman sewer system (Cloaca)? Any *limiting* name will give us that. It is what Moses expects. It is *still* what people expect: our so-called "new atheists" expect it, as they continually try to refute what no Christian asserts—namely, the existence of Mr. Thor or Mrs. Ceres, a deity within the universe and subject to its chances and changes.

"I AM," says the Lord God. It is the name that does not name. "Tell them that I AM sent you"
(see Ex 3:13–14).

Christian philosophers will never have done with contemplating that name and drinking from the inexhaustible fountain of its wisdom. All things that are not God need not be. My existence is not essential to the kind of being I am. I tell my students to consider that if on a certain evening nine months before their birth, the movie on television had been more interesting, they would not exist. From such slender threads of circumstance does our being depend. But God exists necessarily, essentially: He is the One in whom essence and existence are one.

Physicists themselves continually imagine universes in which the laws of our own do not hold, but are different in some way. By that very fact they concede that the laws that govern this universe are *not necessary.* Then this universe itself is *not necessary.* It need not have been. There is nothing about it that requires its existence. It is a very big thing, no doubt. But it is only a thing: finite, contingent, circumscribed in being.

God is. And that is revealed not to philosophers or statesmen or mathematicians, but to the semi-nomadic herdsmen, the Hebrews.

Milton's Satan, escaped from the place called hell, comes to realize that he has not escaped at all:

> *Me miserable! Which way shall I fly*
> *Infinite wrath, or infinite despair?*
> *Which way I fly is Hell: myself am Hell,*
> *And in the lowest deep a lower deep*
> *Still threatening to devour me opens wide,*
> *To which the Hell I suffer seems a Heaven.*

In Marlowe's *Doctor Faustus*, when that would-be necromancer makes light of hell, and says to the demon Mephistopheles that hell must not be any great thing to fear, seeing that Mephistopheles has gotten free of it so easily, the demon replies:

> *Why, this is Hell, nor am I out of it:*
> *Thinkst thou that I, who saw the face of God,*
> *And tasted the eternal joys of heaven,*
> *Am not tormented with ten thousand hells*
> *In being deprived of everlasting bliss?*

Sometimes people who reject the Christian revelation say, with a toss of the head, that it is absurd to believe that God would condemn anyone to hell just because of . . . and then they mention a favorite sin or two, which usually includes their own refusal to worship God Himself. What they fail to see is that by their very testimony they *choose* to be separate from God. The cardinal sins are deadly not because God punishes them extrinsically, as a judge pronouncing sentence upon a thief or a murderer. They are deadly by their nature: they make us into people who would writhe in agony to have to listen to the saints and angels delighting in the glory and the goodness of God. Does that seem incredible? Are there not people who can do no more than snicker uncomfortably in the presence of purity, searching nervously for any small sign that the young people before them are filthy after all?

C. S. Lewis' portrayal of hell, in *The Great Divorce,* reveals the antisocial essence of damnation and the cramped futility, the pettiness, of alienation from God. Hell is a vast gray city, whose buildings are mostly empty, because the inhabitants cannot agree among themselves, and want no more than to put greater and greater distance between them. Thus the city grows endlessly, like a loathsome skin disease. But when its place is viewed from above, in a lush and lovely borderland of heaven, the whole of it seems to occupy no more than the tiniest crack in the earth.

All of which is most fitting. Our word *hell* is related to other words for things that are small and dingy and worthless. It is a grubby *hole* where something beautiful ought to be. It is a dark *hollow* where light and life find no place. A *hell-hole,* then, is something of a redundancy. If it is *hell,* it is a *hole,* and where there is a *hole* instead of something existent that ought to be, there is a bit of *hell.* The word's kinfolk in Latin have to do with hiding: *celare, to cover up;* cf. English *conceal.* That too is fitting.

Hell, for Satan, is a hiding-place from God; and to be in hell is to hide yourself from God, your fellow creatures, and yourself. In this sense we do not march proudly into hell. We skulk and slink and slither into it, all the while pretending that we are great and powerful and brave.

The turning point in the life of the adolescent Dante came, he tells us, when he was walking down the street in Florence and the beautiful Beatrice, accompanied by a couple of other young ladies, approached him in the other direction, and greeted him: *mi saluto*. Literally, she wished him *saluto, health*. It's what we wish when we drink a toast: *Salut!*

When Catholics sing the great Eucharistic hymn, written by Thomas Aquinas, *O Salutaris Hostia*, we sing praise to the *health-giving victim*; so something that is *salutary* is good for what ails us, and a *salubrious* climate, like the dry air of Arizona, is good for the constitution. A *salve* is a cream or ointment that we rub on a wound or a rash, to bring the flesh back to health.

All of these words are related to the Latin adjective *salvus, healthy, hale;* hence also French *sauf*, English *safe*. To confer a permanent health, then, is to *save*: Latin *salvare;* and that health never to be lost is Latin *salvatio:* English *salvation*. When I was a college student, the company I worked for organized a great rap session for us youngsters, which included our having to choose which of a dozen or so desirable nouns we valued the most. One of those was *salvation*. Of course I chose that one, because there could be nothing greater than that. Yet the pretty girl next to me could not understand why. She didn't think it was foolish. It just made no sense to her. Perhaps it would have made more sense if I had explained that it meant the ultimate in health, flourishing, life.

The very name of our Savior means just that: *God saves*. Or, to reveal the inner meaning of each part of the Holy Name of Jesus: *I AM brings health;* our health is in the name of Him Who is.

To what shall we liken brothers dwelling together in harmony? The Psalmist says that it is like *oil* running down the beard of Aaron, plentiful and rich, oil that spills upon his robes. Or to what shall we liken what it means to be led by the saving Lord? "You have prepared for me a table in the sight of my enemies," says David; "you have anointed my head with oil; my cup brims over" (see Ps 23:5). When, during a great famine, the prophet Elijah asked the widow with the young son to give him something to eat, she replied that she had only a little flour left, and a little oil in her jar. But Elijah told her to gather some sticks and make a fire, and bake a few cakes for herself, her son, and him, and she would never lack for flour, and her jar of oil would never run dry. She did so, and she and her son never went hungry again (see 1 Kings 17:5).

It is hard for us to imagine how important *oil* was in the Mediterranean world. For us, the word suggests anything that is slippery: so we have *petroleum, rock-oil,* for our automobiles and other machines; and we have *oily* politicians, whose palms are *greased* with the money of the rich. But the people in that place and time used the *olive,* from which we derive our word *oil,* for food and for cooking and for light, for cleaning the body (lye soap was invented later, up north, from animal fat), for perfumes (all based on oil), and for healing remedies. That is why one of the first things the Jesuit missionaries in the Southwest did was to introduce the olive tree, and to teach the Indians how to use the olive press. It was a crucial step towards making them independent and able to dwell in self-sufficient agricultural villages.

The Hebrew word we transcribe as *Messiah* means, literally, the *Anointed One;* translated into Greek, *Christos.* The prophet Samuel anointed the lad David, to become the second king of Israel, and God promised David that his house would reign forever. That has come to pass through Jesus the Anointed High Priest and King, Jesus the Son of David, our "king and priest and sacrifice," as the well-known carol puts it. When we are anointed with chrism in the Sacrament of Confirmation, we are ushered into the fullness of Christ's priesthood: each of us is to become as it were a *microchristos, a little Christ.* That is what happens to Spenser's Knight of the Red Cross on the night of the second day of his climactic fight with the dragon. He falls backwards, unconscious, near a special tree, the Tree of Life:

From that first Tree forth flowed, as from a Well,
A trickling Stream of Balm, most sovereign
And dainty dear, which on the Ground still fell,
And overflowed all the fertile Plain,

As it had dewed been with timely Rain:
Life and long Health that gracious Ointment gave,
And deadly Wounds could heal, and rear again
The senseless Corse appointed for the Grave.
Into that same he fell, which did from Death him
save.

He rises up on the morning of the third day, utterly healed and made new, so that the Dragon is not sure whether it is even the same fellow, or a "new-made" knight. It is both, of course: it is the Knight of the Red Cross, and it is a new knight. He slays the dragon at the first thrust. His name, and the name of every human being who is saved, is Christ. "For it is not I," says Saint Paul, "but Christ who works in me" (see Gal 2:20).

pure

"Blessed are the pure in heart," says Jesus, "for they shall see God" (see Mt 5:8). If we think we know what that means, we should consider the final words of the final prophet of the Old Testament in the stirring English of the King James. It is Malachi, referring to the great and terrifying day when the Lord will send his messenger before him: "But who may abide the day of his coming? and who shall stand when he appeareth? for he is like a refiner's fire, and like fullers' soap: And he shall sit as a refiner and purifier of silver: and he shall purify the sons of Levi, and purge them as gold and silver, that

they may offer unto the Lord an offering in righteousness" (Mal 3:2–3). Handel worked those verses into his
Messiah: And He shall purify.

Fire destroys, says Saint Augustine, but fire also puri-
fies. If you want to clear away the dross from gold or silver ore, you melt it in a fire that is so hot that it separates
the precious metal from the dross, which is lighter, and
which will float like scum upon the molten gold or silver.
You clear it away, and what is left then is *pure.*

That is how we should view *purgatory:* it is the place
where sinners are made *pure.* Dante constructs his *Purgatorio* as a seven-terraced mountain in the South Seas,
opposite from Calvary on the globe. As you travel up the
road that winds about the mountain, at each terrace you
atone for one of the seven deadly sins, beginning with
pride and ending with lust. If the reader is waiting for fire,
though, he will be disappointed, until the last terrace of
all, where the souls walk about in a fire that is so hot, you
would find it cool to be thrown into boiling glass. Dante
himself must cross through that fire, the fire that he
says *refines;* and only the prospect of seeing his beloved
Beatrice suffices to persuade him to enter it.

We do not want our foul sins "to be burnt and
purged away," as the ghost of Hamlet's father puts it,
and there is a simple reason for that. Fire hurts. The
fuller's lye that the prophet refers to can only work
if it eats into the grime on the cloth. The fuller's lye
of penitence works by eating into the sins that have
soaked deep into our flesh and our souls. The question is not why it should hurt, but how we could possibly expect that it would not hurt. But there is a hurt
that somehow feels good to us, and that characterizes
the suffering of the souls in the *Purgatorio.* Dante's

brother-in-law Forese calls it *our punishment,* and then immediately corrects himself: *our solace.*

There is not much talk these days about the virtue of *purity.* I suspect it is too hot for us. It stings, like the fuller's lye, like bleach, like the touch of fire.

When the souls of the damned gather upon the shores of the dismal River Acheron, Charon the boatman, pushing his little skiff across the water by a long pole he plants in the mud, greets them with these words:

> *"Guai a voi, anime prave!*
> *Non isperate mai veder lo cielo.*
> *I' vegno per menarvi all'altra riva*
> *nelle tenebre etterne, in caldo e 'n gelo."*
> *"Woe to you, crooked souls!*
> *Give up all hope to see the skies again.*
> *I come to lead you to the other shore,*
> *into eternal darkness, fire and ice."*

I've translated the Italian *cielo, heaven,* as *skies,* which the word also means. I wanted to stress the horrible constriction of hell, that prison with a low ceiling (cf. French *ciel, heaven, sky*) over the soul of man. I ask my students how long it would take for them to go quite mad, if they were told they must live out their days indoors, never to see the sky. They tell me they would last a week or so. Man is always more than man: we must aspire to the transcendent, or we die inside.

In most languages, the word for *sky* does double service for *heaven*, that transcendent place and state of being which Christians and Jews understand as looking upon the face of God. It is natural for us to "locate" that place by looking upwards, although, as Augustine observed, there's the *heaven* above our heads, which is just a part of the physical universe, and the *heaven of heavens*, which is beyond. In any case, Hebrew *shamayim*, Greek *ouranos*, Latin *caelum*, Italian *cielo*, French *ciel*, German *Himmel*, and Welsh *nefoedd* all signify either the skies or heaven, according to context. English is the odd man out.

We have our word *sky*, probably coming to us, like most of our *sk-* words, from the Vikings invading the north and east of England. We also have *heaven*, from Old English *heofon*, pronounced *heh-uh-vun*, which used to do that same double duty, although there was another word, *weolcen*, *weh-ul-kun*, denoting that blue vault above us, whence we have the archaic *welkin* (cf. German *Woelken*, *clouds*). In Welsh the movement seems to have proceeded in the opposite direction, from an old word for clouds (cf. Latin *nebula*) to *nefoedd*, *skies*, *heaven*. None of this is surprising. But English, by the historical accidents that give us our language so rich in words, reveals the distinction that the theologians and the poets have long understood. The sky is one thing, but heaven is another.

And that, my friends, *heaven*, is as good a place as any other to end this book . . . and the only place to conclude the book, made up of thoughts, words, and deeds, that constitutes one's life. God willing, may we all meet there one day in friendship of the truest sort.

ACKNOWLEDGMENTS

I wish to express my gratitude here to all of the men and women, some of whom have passed away, who ever taught me about the languages I know: Sister Felician Grogan; Professors George Kane, Aldo Scaglione, Kenneth Reckford, Sarah Mack, Ennio Rao, Joseph Wittig, and especially Harry Solo, whose courses in Old English and the history of the English language were a perfect delight. I am also indebted to the wonderfully instructive website of Douglas Harper, *www.etymonline.com*, a romp through English and its relations. *The Oxford English Dictionary*, of course, remains the gold standard of etymological and historical research into English words.

Additionally, I would like to acknowledge the many "friends of years" quoted liberally throughout these pages, masters of language whose written words inspired in me from my youth a love of words that shows no sign of abating: John Milton, William Shakespeare, Aristophanes, Edmund Spenser, Christopher Marlowe, Hilaire Belloc, and, of course, Dante Aligheri, among others. I would be remiss if I did not remember here that oft-forgotten, many-faceted storyteller and poet, Anonymous.

Further thanks are due to those luminaries of American sporting and popular culture such as Bob Gibson and Boris Badunov, not to mention Atanasio "Tony" Perez and the always entertaining Lily Munster. Would that such giants still populated the American cultural landscape.

ANSWERS TO QUIZZES

Quiz One

1. The initial *s* on *square* needs some splainin'. In Italian, the initial Latin prefix *dis-* was usually abbreviated to a single consonant, *s-*, giving Italian some very unusual ways to begin a word: *dis-boccare > sboccare, to spill from the mouth; dis-graziato > sgraziato, disgraced,* and so on. Something divided up into four was *disquadratum > squadrato,* coming into English through French as *square.* So it is related to *quarter, one fourth. Queer,* meaning *crooked,* is the oddball, as is fitting.

2. English *day* is not related to Latin *dies, day,* or to Greek *dios, divine, shining > Zeus,* the sky-god. The latter are related. *Daily* is out. But Latin *diurnus* becomes Italian *giorno* and French *jour,* so *journal* and *journey* (initially, a day's travel) would be in.

3. Latin words beginning with *p* correspond with English words beginning with *f*, as Grimm's Law tells us: *pater, father; piscis, fish; pes, foot.* Here *pork* is from Norman French, who made the English whom they had conquered serve it to them from the pigs they butchered. The Old English word for a boar was *fearh*, related to Latin *porcus;* it becomes our old word *farrow*, meaning *piglet. Pig* is the pig here.

4. Latin students know that some superlative adjectives do not take the main suffix *-issimus;* some have *-errimus* or *-illimus.* Proto-Germanic had a superlative suffix in *-m-* that was eventually displaced almost entirely by the suffix we all know and love: *-est.* But in one word the suffix survived: the word that meant that you were in front, *feor* (cf. English *first, fore*). So if you were in front of everybody, you were *feorma.* But after a while people no longer understood that word as a superlative. So they added the new suffixes to it, producing words that give us *former* and *foremost.* Those are closely related. A similar thing happened to the ancestor of the word *most,* which shows up once in a while in Shakespeare as *moe,* meaning *a lot. Most* here is out.

5. Can you be *hostile* to a *guest?* Macbeth could. You never know who's going to show up at your door, or what the guy who runs the Bates Hotel is up to. That explains how Latin *hostis, enemy,* could also be your *host,* and why it's not so far a stretch to see that it is related to Old English *gast, guest* (for the consonants, compare: *hortis, garden; haedus, goat; habere, give*). And what's the worst sort

of creature who can appear in the basement on a bad night? Sure, a *ghost*. The *h* doesn't belong in that word, nor does that word belong in the trio. Out, damned Spot!

6. Most English words with the diphthong *oi* *(oy)* come to us from Norman French, and *foil* and *boil* are among them. They are, however, not related. *Foil* (Modern French *feuille;* and if you can pronounce that, *plus de pouvoir a toi*) comes from Latin *folium, leaf;* hence *gold foil,* or *gold leaf,* which is gold beaten to an airy thinness—same thing with *aluminum foil,* but not so pretty. *Boil* comes through French from the Latin *bullire, to bubble. Bole* is an original English word, meaning *leaf,* and is a cousin of *folium* (for the consonants, compare: *frater, brother; fagus, beech; flare, blow*). Lance that *boil.*

7. "Like a shepherd He feeds his flock," says the prophet. Latin *pastor, shepherd,* is literally the man who protects and *feeds* the sheep. Yes, Latin *pascor, I feed,* is related to the ancient Germanic word that gives us *food, feed, fodder,* and so on. A *farmer* might easily have been a *firmer,* if the vowel had fallen the other way: a man who rents land by a fixed contract.

8. Our word *ring* was once *hring,* with a hard *h,* related to Latin *c* (compare: *caput, head; cor, heart*). So it is related to Latin *circum, around,* and to the various words built from it, like *circle* and *circumference* and *circumnavigate. Round* is out.

9. Sometimes the speakers of the Romance languages adopted Germanic words, and pronounced them as made sense to them in their languages. People

from Spain and Italy and France did not have words beginning with our semivowel, *w*. So they heard it differently; and put a rounded *g* before the rounded *w*. Try it; you can hear how it would happen. So Walter is Italian *Gualtieri*, French *Gautier;* and *war* is Italian *guerra*, pronounced *gwehr-rah,* French *guerre*, and Spanish *guerro*. *Guerilla* is from Spanish. *Worth* here isn't.

10. I've heard all my life from pulpits that *communion* has to do with *union*. It doesn't. The two *m*'s give the game away. You are in *com-munion* with someone if you share the same *moenera, walls,* and the same duties that go along with protecting the walls. *Union* comes ultimately from Latin *unus, one,* which is a cousin of Old English *an, one* (cf. German *ein*). Our indefinite article *a* is an abbreviated and unstressed form of *an. Communion* is kicked out.

....

Quiz Two

1. True. Compare with German *zu,* which means both *to* and *too.*
2. False. A *pale* is a fence: *paling, palisades.*
3. True.
4. False. We have to bring out the hidden *s: ex-specto, to look out.*
5. False. The similarities are coincidental. Ultimately from the Greek *Pergamon,* near the site of old Troy, where parchment was reputed to have been invented.
6. True. Compare with Italian, *mi piace, it pleases me.*

7. True.
8. True. Compare with German *unkaemmt, uncombed.*
9. False. We have no idea where *prissy* comes from. *Pristine* means *in its original form,* as of a coin new minted.
10. False. Latin *sexus* is related to words having to do with divisions.

....

Quiz Three

1. Yes, and well attested in the best writers as late as the eighteenth century.
2. No. A modern invention.
3. Yes. Note the fighting song of the Levellers, seventeenth century communists:
   When Adam delved and Eve span, Who was then the gentleman?
4. Yes. Shakespeare uses it in the phrase "Pharaoh's lean kine," the seven emaciated cows that the Pharaoh dreamed of, interpreted by Joseph as seven coming years of famine.
5. Yes. The villain: our buddy *metathesis of r,* meaning that *r* often switches places with a vowel.
6. No. The child's mistake by analogy with *sang, rang, drank,* and so on.
7. No. Originally there was no word *bust.* That is a recent slang form of *burst.*
8. No. Just a joke.
9. No. *Mend* comes from Latin through French, and so takes the standard past tense ending, *-ed.*

10. No. If we kept the true original, we'd be saying *one lamb, two lamber.*

....

Quiz Four

1. True. His slenderer brother Lloyd Waner was then called "Little Poison." They didn't like the nicknames.
2. False. *Bum* in the first sense is fairly recent, and has to do with walking around, loafing: cf. German *bummeln.* The other, *the bottom,* is much older, and is attested in Shakespeare's *Measure for Measure,* in the character of Pompey Bum.
3. True.
4. True.
5. False. No relation at all. *Jibber-Jabber* is imitative, and *algebra* comes from Arabic.
6. False. Oh, they might use the smelling salts, but *the vapors* are the gases that were supposed to have risen from your bowels and gotten into your brain.
7. True. The four "humors" were bodily fluids that marked you with a certain personality: black bile (melancholic), yellow bile (choleric), blood (sanguine), and phlegm (phlegmatic).
8. True. Poke is another way of saying pouch.
9. True. Gut is still a live nautical term.
10. False. *Ye* is the original second person plural pronoun, in the nominative case. The accusative, *you,* took over its role, as it took over the role of the singular, causing us a lot of needless confusion.

Spread the Faith with . . .

TAN·BOOKS

A Division of Saint Benedict Press, LLC

TAN books are powerful tools for evangelization. They lift the mind to God and change lives. Millions of readers have found in TAN books and booklets an effective way to teach and defend the Faith, soften hearts, and grow in prayer and holiness of life.

Throughout history the faithful have distributed Catholic literature and sacramentals to save souls. St. Francis de Sales passed out his own pamphlets to win back those who had abandoned the Faith. Countless others have distributed the Miraculous Medal to prompt conversions and inspire deeper devotion to God. Our customers use TAN books in that same spirit.

If you have been helped by this or another TAN title, share it with others. Become a TAN Missionary and share our life changing books and booklets with your family, friends and community. We'll help by providing special discounts for books and booklets purchased in quantity for purposes of evangelization. Write or call us for additional details.

TAN Books
Attn: TAN Missionaries Department
PO Box 410487
Charlotte, NC 28241

Toll-free (800) 437-5876
missionaries@TANBooks.com

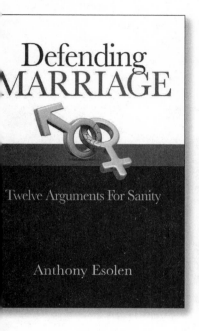
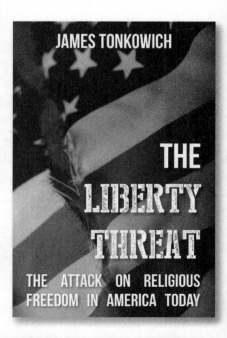

TAN·CLASSICS

A collection of the finest literature in the Catholic tradition.

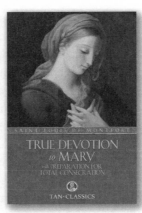

978-0-89555-227-3

978-0-89555-154-2

978-0-89555-155-9

Our TAN Classics collection is a well-balanced sampling
of the finest literature in the Catholic tradition.

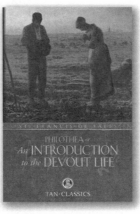

978-0-89555-230-3

978-0-89555-228-0

978-0-89555-151-1

TAN·BOOKS

The SPIRITUAL EXERCISES
of SAINT IGNATIUS *at* MANRESA

TAN·CLASSICS

978-0-89555-153-5

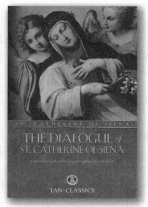

THE DIALOGUE *of*
ST. CATHERINE OF SIENA

TAN·CLASSICS

978-0-89555-149-8

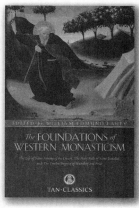

The FOUNDATIONS *of*
WESTERN MONASTICISM

TAN·CLASSICS

978-0-89555-199-3

The collection includes distinguished spiritual works of
the saints, philosophical treatises and famous biographies.

ABANDONMENT *to*
DIVINE PROVIDENCE

TAN·CLASSICS

978-0-89555-226-6

The SPIRITUAL COMBAT
and A TREATISE ON
PEACE OF SOUL

TAN·CLASSICS

978-0-89555-152-8

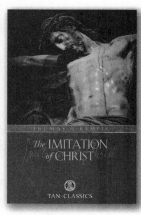

The IMITATION
of CHRIST

TAN·CLASSICS

978-0-89555-225-9

Visit us at TANBooks.com

TAN·BOOKS

TAN Books is the Publisher You Can Trust With Your Faith.

TAN Books was founded in 1967 to preserve the spiritual, intellectual, and liturgical traditions of the Catholic Church. At a critical moment in history TAN kept alive the great classics of the Faith and drew many to the Church. In 2008 TAN was acquired by Saint Benedict Press. Today TAN continues to teach and defend the Faith to a new generation of readers.

TAN publishes more than 600 booklets, Bibles, and books. Popular subject areas include theology and doctrine, prayer and the supernatural, history, biography, and the lives of the saints. TAN's line of educational and homeschooling resources is featured at TANHomeschool.com.

TAN publishes under several imprints, including TAN, Neumann Press, ACS Books, and the Confraternity of the Precious Blood. Sister imprints include Saint Benedict Press, Catholic Courses, and Catholic Scripture Study.

**For more information about TAN,
or to request a free catalog, visit
TANBooks.com**

**Or call us toll-free at
(800) 437-5876**